Clarify Simplify Amplify

Clarify Simplify Amplify

A COACH-APPROACH TO MAKING YOUR DREAMS COME TRUE

GARY L. CRAWFORD

FREILING
PUBLISHING

Published by Freiling Publishing, a division of Freiling Agency, LLC.

70 Main Street, Suite 23-MEC
Warrenton, VA 20186

www.FreilingPublishing.com

Designed by Grade Design and Adeline Media, London

ISBN 978-1-950948-25-3

Printed in the United States of America

CONTENTS

**OTHER BOOKS BY
GARY L. CRAWFORD**

Praise for
Clarify Simplify Amplify

Dr. Gary Crawford has masterfully woven a case study with proven coaching principles. The book deals with practical application rather than theoretical ideas, setting his work apart from many authors in the field of coaching. By taking a small business through step-by-step practical procedures that produced tangible results, this coach-approach led a business through real life demands that included personnel and cash-flow management. I highly recommend this book for any entrepreneurial minded person who wants to achieve his or her maximum potential.

Bill Price

Impact Stewardship Resources, Founder

One does not read far until the theme becomes crystal clear, a book that overwhelmingly informs so that you may be surprisingly transformed. Gary writes in hopes that the reader will be so impacted, that they in return, will become the leader they desire to be. As a leader you then in return, develop (coach) others.

Johnny Hunt

Senior Vice President of Evangelism and Leadership for the North American Mission Board

Pastor Emeritus, First Baptist Church Woodstock, Georgia

When I received this manuscript from Gary Crawford, I armed myself with a pen and a highlighter. As with nearly every experience I have with him, I knew that there would be some significant insights to be gleaned. I was not disappointed. I found myself quickly jotting down quotes and ideas from this book that I can use and apply to my life both personally and professionally.

All throughout this book, Gary is intentional with serving nuggets of wisdom and principles that can apply to any situation, personally or corporately. The case study in the book, of a familiar American franchise, showcases the pivotal moments on a journey of growth and change for those involved.

The "coach approach", as described throughout this book is not just a leadership style, it is a paradigm rooted in best thinking, best experiences and best practices that have come from a life dedicated to loving and serving people.

By the end of reading this work, I can honestly say that this book embodies a large part of *who* Gary Crawford has been to me; Instructional, Educational and Inspiring.

Daniel Morris

Pastor, Whispering Valley Church

Nashville, TN

Want to discover and live your dreams? If so, this book is a must read. I've known the author, Gary Crawford, for a number of years and he is the real deal. He's not only discovered & lived out his own dreams he's helped many others do so as well. He's done so in the context of being a pastor of a large church, as a pioneering leader in global missions and as an Executive Coach to successful business leaders. In his book, Clarify Simplify Amplify, you can discover the step by step process that you too, can live out your dreams.

Jeff Rogers
ForbesBooks featured author of *Create a Thriving Family Legacy: How to share your Wisdom and Wealth with your Children and Grandchildren*
Founder & CEO of Stewardship Legacy Coaching and
Stewardship Advisory Group

Required reading for every leader wanting to develop a strong leadership team. You will discover an insightful, straight-forward, practical application for daily team growth towards successful transformational relationships instead of the transactional interaction of our current day. Follow as Gary encourages an actual team of leaders through each coaching principle to tap into their greater confidence and success.

Douglas R. Medlin
Stewardship Advisor, International Mission Board

As a high energy leader who manages a team to accomplish aggressive goals, this book greatly challenges me. A life of intentionality lies not only in our ability to answer tough questions, but rather in having a coach who asks the right questions at the right time. The author provides both clarity and encouragement on how to move towards a desired future and

I look forward to sharing Gary Crawford's coach approach to influence others.

Melissa Allen
University of Florida, Director of UF Online Enrollment Services
Global Missions 365, Director of Development

This book has a great flow and goes way beyond concepts in coaching to a lived-out-praxis. The content is timely, practical, professional. It brought joy to my heart as I read it. The underlying theme woven through the entire book is TRUST. As the team developed, we see trust as the marker that scribed the mission, vision, purpose statements, and plans of the team on the whiteboard of their lives.

Robert Shettler, D.Min.

I've known Gary for over 20 years, and I've seen in his life what he has penned in this book. He is a man of character, integrity, and is trustworthy to lead any organization or group through a coaching process. His leadership capacities and skills have always helped him to motivate others to be their very best. He asks insightful questions that may make you uncomfortable initially but are simply designed to help you decide how to move forward to the goals and purpose that you've set for yourself. He wants to see everyone grow both personally and professionally. This book, and ultimately time with Gary, will help the reader on his journey to excel in any endeavor.

Jeff Singerman PhD
Cross Cultural Missionary & Mission Strategist
International Mission Board

Dr. Crawford has a dynamic, effective, and unique way of thinking that motivates. He presents a creative team approach for the importance of core values, clear vision and mission. I learned new techniques of engagement for productivity and team effectiveness through his coach-approach. Want to build an effective team in ministry or in the corporate world? Want to make your dreams come true? This book will show you how!

Cesar Parra

Missions Strategist

Canadian National Baptist Convention

Dr. Gary Crawford deeply desires for *you* to get to where *you* want to go - by skillfully asking discovery questions to help you unveil your dreams. His passion is to guide the coachee to "self-reveal" and achieve their dream. Together they celebrate dreams-come-true.

Scott Thomas, Ph.D.

Vice-President of Figura Enterprises, LLC.

"What are you afraid of?" was the question Gary Crawford asked me over 15 years ago during a time when I was fighting against the "call" that would change my world. His question unlocked the one thing that would keep me from living God's dream for my life.

Leadership and coaching are deeply intuitive for Gary and the fruits of his gifting echoes around the globe through his intentionality, wisdom and genuine love for people. Who could have thought that a journey of discovery would allow that once twenty-year-old girl to sort out her purpose, her dreams and live them out courageously!

Through these years, with God's grace, and clarity of purpose, I've been fulfilling my dream by directing a Brazilian NGO that brings change to thousands of people in the Amazon basin.

It is an absolute treasure to see the truths and principles that changed my life now available to others in this book, *Clarity Simplify Amplify*. A perfect combination of faith and a strategic approach to life. His book is inspiring, practical, biblical, and it might yet bring about the very best in your life!

Sarah Rodriguez
National Director, Justice and Mercy – Amazon

Dedication

D edicated to Ray Holloway and the courageous team who engaged the coaching process, took the risk, did the hard work, experienced their dreams coming true, and demonstrated unmistakably the power of leadership coaching.

Acknowledgments

A t the end of the day, I want to serve my family by whatever I am doing. In the context of this book, I would hope to encourage them all that their own dreams can come true even in the midst of the realities of lost dreams in a broken world. They remain my most precious treasure.

My wife Ingrid is a positive and persistent encouragement and support in my personal and professional growth. The incredible accomplishments, including the travel in seventeen countries the last 30 months, could not have happened without her initiative, support, and constant smile.

Working with Ray Holloway and the team has been a highlight of my coaching experience. I have been challenged by them and learned from them. They have added immeasurably to my own dreams coming true.

A book can be written with a pen in hand, but publishing is a different story. Many thanks to Natalie Rose and the StoryTerrace team for walking with me each step of the way to get this visionary experience to your reading.

We all have risen on the shoulders of those stronger than us and who are ahead of us. That has certainly been true for me as I have learned and grown over the years. Thank you to all.

Thank you, the reader, for making the choice to join me on this journey. And for those of you who, believing in the value of this book, share it with a loved one, friend, neighbor or colleague, who you think can be informed and encouraged. Thank you!

Foreword

by Ray Holloway
Owner and Operator,
Chick-fil-A Archer Road

Effectively leading an organization can be incredibly rewarding – especially when that organization is a Chick-fil-A restaurant. However, there's no doubt that leading a group of 140+ employees with excellence has its own leadership challenges. I am truly grateful for my fellow Chick-fil-A Operators, who allow me to learn from them and explore new ideas with them. About two years ago, another Operator and I were sharing and exchanging ideas, when I learned that he had enlisted an executive coach to work with him and his lead team. Curious about this concept and its effectiveness, I asked a number of questions, contemplating if coaching would be beneficial for my current team. This began my search for executive leadership coaches in my area. That's when I found Gary Crawford Leadership.

Formerly, Gary Crawford served as a pastor at a church that my parents attended. I had visited with them several times over the years and met Gary. When I learned that Gary had transitioned from senior pastor after 34 years to executive leadership coaching, I knew he was the one to coach my team. Not only my team, but myself as a leader and business owner. I realized I needed his help with not only my professional development but also with my personal and spiritual development. Once Gary and I sat down to discuss my needs and wants, I knew that he was the coach for us. It was then that Chick-fil-A Archer Road began the journey through the coach-approach process.

Gary came and met the team. They instantly felt encouraged and cared for. Here was someone who's primary focus was to support and develop them. Little did they know of the challenges he would place in front of them. These challenges stretched each member of the team - and myself - for the better.

Trust. In this book you will see 'trust' as the foundational principle that guided everything else. In our team's transformation you will find that Gary had a very effective way of exploring trust levels between team members. He taught us how to break down any areas of mistrust and grow together for effective teamwork and productivity.

Gary, with his technique of Clarify – Simplify – Amplify, helped us hone who we were, what our purpose was, and what we wanted to accomplish. I found this experience to be challenging, yet extremely rewarding. While this is beneficial for any individual, its positive results are multiplied when done together as a team. Just imagine - a whole team of people learning who they are, what their personal 'why' is, and a way to get there. I challenge you to read this book, follow the steps outlined and be prepared for personal and professional transformation. Just one caution, you will have to apply yourself to the work. *Real transformation* comes with *real work.*

Why and How to Read This Book for Transformational Change

"In the case of good books, the point is not to see how many of them you can get through, but rather how many can get through to you."
— *Mortimer J. Adler, American philosopher and educator*

R eading books has so many benefits. Surely you've been told that "reading is good for you." Now, research backs up what we inherently know to be true. Sadie Trombetta, in an article entitled, "What Does Reading Do to Your Brain? These Five Effects Are Pretty Astounding," writes, "Over the years, doctors, scientists, and researchers have confirmed that reading is a stress-reducing activity that can lower your heart rate and blood pressure. It's been proven to improve people's memories, increase brain power, and even enhance empathic skills. Reading has even been linked to longer life spans." I encourage you to read this article about the fascinating results of reading (Trombetta 2017). However, my point is this—reading *this* book can have an amazing influence in your life. Perhaps it will even be a "pivotal moment" on your journey of growth.

There are various ways that you may read this book:

- a cursory reading where you scan and look at overall concepts or specific information. This may serve a purpose for you.

- an attentive reading when you set aside time and read systematically through the book. This will give you a better grasp on how this book can be helpful to you personally and professionally.
- a serious reading when you not only read carefully but with the objective of learning and effectively applying the process and principles to implement personal and/or professional change, maybe even transformational change, as you will read about in this book.

I encourage you to read the book in the way that best serves *your purpose* for reading. This is how I try to maximize the potential benefit of every book now in my growing library of over 4,000 volumes. Read first about the author. This will reveal background experiences, possible biases, values, skills, worldview, and life perspective. This will help you understand the author's writing, intent, and hoped-for contributions to the reader.

Second, read any material outside the main body of the book, such as the foreword, preface, prologue, introduction, and epilogue. This will give you, as the reader, an even broader view of the author and the book's objectives.

Third, you may find it helpful to highlight, underline, or otherwise notate that which is most helpful to you. I use the following simple notation system to assist me in absorbing a book:

! I agree
? I don't understand
→ apply now
R resource
I insight

When possible, I do a quick review of my notations and summarize the most important ones in the back of the book. This allows me to quickly reference what is most significant and thus increases the usefulness of the book in my everyday experience. I have collected books that have had such an impact on my life that I return to read them again and again. In addition, I date each book in the front when I begin to read, and date in the back when I finish, adding the time and location when I complete the final page. I have dated books with location references from around the world. This makes for good memories. Incidentally, much of my reading over the years has occurred while traveling or waiting for appointments.

Finally, I always ask, "With whom might I share this book?" A particular book may be more helpful to one person than another. I seek to align the book recommendation with the interest and the needs of the person. As a follower of Christ, this is a matter of prayer as well. Passing forward a good book is one way to care for others and increase influence.

The principle here is to be *intentional*, and read with the end in mind. This will ensure you benefit the most from your investment in purchase and time.

This being said, it is my earnest hope that this book will be a "defining" investment for you. May it create a "pivotal moment" that will move you toward your dream and increase your ability to work as a catalyst in helping the dreams of others come true as well.

If you are a more serious reader, you will find at the end of each chapter three questions for personal and professional impact. The questions can be used individually or in a group setting. The hope is that by engaging these questions you will understand the next step you need for growth and forward movement. In doing so, we become who we have never been and do what we have never done!

The famous author C.S. Lewis (2019) put it this way: "Those of us who have been true readers all our life seldom fully realize the enormous extension of our being which we owe to authors," he says. "We realize it best when we talk with an unliterary friend. He may be full of goodness and good sense, but he inhabits a tiny world. In it, we should be suffocated. The man who is content to be only himself, and therefore less a self, is in prison. My own eyes are not enough for me, I will see through those of others. Reality, even seen through the eyes of many, is not enough. I will see what others have invented."

★ ★ ★

"I read a book one day and my whole life was changed."
— Orhan Pamuk, 2006 Nobel Peace Prize winner

The Case for Executive Coaching

"Research does demonstrate that one-on-one executive coaching is of value."
— *F. Turner, Ph.D.*

"Does coaching work? Yes. Good coaches provide a truly important service. They tell you the truth when no one else will."
— *Jack Welch, former CEO General Electric*

"The Manchester survey of 140 companies shows nine in ten executives believe coaching to be worth their time and dollars. The average return was more than $5 for each spent."
— *The Denver Post*

"Corporations believe that coaching helps keep employees and that the dollar investment in it is far less than the cost of replacing an employee."
— *David A. Thomas Fitzhugh,*
professor of Business Administration,
Harvard Business School

"Recent studies show business coaching and executive coaching to be the most effective means for achieving sustainable growth, change and development in the individual, group and organization."

— HR Monthly

"Across corporate America, coaching sessions at many companies have become as routine for executives as budget forecasts and quota meetings."

— Investors Business Daily

"Coaching takes a holistic view of the individual: work, corporate values, personal needs and career development are made to work in synergy, not against one another."

— British Journal of Administrative Management

"Career management coaches can identify missing skills or style difficulties and other pragmatic tips."

— The New York Times

"If you want to build your business and at the same time have a rewarding personal life, you call a coach."

—The Denver Post

"Using coaching instead of sending executives and managers to seminars two or three times a year can be more beneficial to ongoing career development, not to mention less expensive…"

— PC Week

"Who exactly seeks out a coach? Winners who want more out of life."

— Chicago Tribune

"I absolutely believe that people, unless coached, never reach their maximum capabilities."

— Bob Nardelli, former CEO, Home Depot

Preface
From There to Anywhere

"Your visions will become clear only when you can look into your own heart. Who looks outside, dreams; who looks inside, awakes."

— *Carl Jung*

I'm from Providence. No, not the well-known Providence, Rhode Island, but a little village in North Central Florida. You know the kind of small town I'm talking about: population 300 (maybe), a general store on the one main street, a gas station (with an attendant who washed your windshield and checked the air in your tires!), and a feed store. Still, for such a small place, it was certainly a busy place, and it was home to some good, hardworking folks, the kind who make a great community.

My dad grew up during the Great Depression and, against considerable odds, he became a successful businessman with a strong work ethic. My mom worked long hours by his side, until her life was cut short at age 34. I had two younger sisters and a cousin who was more like a brother. When my mother passed away, our world came crashing down.

I spent my formative years as a fair-haired, insecure boy in this rural country setting. My dad had multiple businesses, so I worked in the fields in "row crop" agriculture and also behind the counter at the general store. Store work was the job I liked least, because it kept me inside. In the midst of "work first," "don't call in, crawl in" work mentality, there was school. School was important, but the expectation was to get it done without letting it interfere with work. So, it's not surprising that I struggled academically, and my involvement with sports was very limited.

My world was small, although looking back, not as small as I thought at the time. Our idea of excitement was a trip to the creek, or lake, for swimming, camping, or skiing. The only movie I remember seeing in town was *Hatari* starring John Wayne. I know, you're thinking "how deprived!" However, we attended church fairly regularly in a different county than where we lived, which expanded my social opportunities.

Dreams as real possibilities were hard to come by. Losing Mom changed everything. It was hard to see "beyond the end of the row," "over the fence," or "past the bend in the road," so to speak, to see a preferred future where I could meet well-traveled people of stature, accomplishment, academic acumen, and financial means. That possibility seemed more like fantasy. Unattainable. And I felt so incapable, incompetent, maybe even unworthy.

Yet, there was a voice within me like the sirens in Herman Melville's *Moby Dick*, luring me. It was a different voice I would discover later that, rather than luring me, led me—not to crash on the rocks as in Greek mythology, but to experiences way beyond the horizon I knew at the time. There was within me a spark, a glimmer of hope for something different, something more, that I could not visualize at the time. But I knew it was out there, like Wendell Berry's description of his life.

"If you could do it, I suppose, it would be a good idea to live your life in a straight line…But that is not the way I have done it, so far. I am a pilgrim, but my pilgrimage has been wandering and unmarked. Often, I did not know where I was going until I was already there. I have had my share of desires and goals, but my life has come to me, or I have gone to it, mainly by way of mistakes and surprises. I am an ignorant pilgrim, crossing a dark valley. And yet for a long time, looking back, I have been unable to shake off the feeling that I have been led——make of that what you will."

Up until age eighteen, that described my experience. That voice, that glimmer, that beckoning, vague as it was, held steady, and it confronted the fears and insecurities inside me. They did battle. They still do. There was the tension between the world I knew and the world I wanted to know——and the chasm I would have to cross to get there. It seemed formidable. It would prove to be so.

I remember a momentary dialogue with my dad as he was standing in the doorway of our home, about to leave. The brief conversation was about college. I remarked, "I don't want my family relationships and values to change, but I want to become more and do more." He replied, "You won't (change your values), and you will (become and do more)." He wanted that for me. That's why he encouraged me toward dentistry. He knew it would require another level of academic achievement, but in the end it would provide me with a good income and an enjoyable lifestyle.

At that time, I couldn't clarify my dream (purpose, aspiration, ambition), articulate my vision, and I certainly could not design a strategy. But somewhere within me lay buried the embryonic awareness that would one day give birth to a dream come true.

Looking over my shoulder, I see now that dream was nurtured in the womb of the faith of an eleven-year-old boy who had a personal encounter with Jesus Christ. Christ revealed His unconditional love for me and assured me He had a plan and purpose for my life. That dream would include a life of helping others discover, accomplish, and live their God-given dreams. Now, as an adult, I state my life purpose this way: "As a follower of Christ I will love well, and be an adventurer and pilgrim who treads uncharted waters; as I inspire, communicate, and coach, I will encourage others to do the same."

As I was writing this, I laid my pen aside to make an appointment with a young man, Gavin Rollins, who is pursuing his dream. Raised in a Christian home of missionary parents, he learned about the dream and leadership of Joseph in Egypt. He read about heroes like General Robert E. Lee and Ulysses S. Grant, who led our civil war armies in the war that set destiny for our nation; Jim Elliott, missionary and martyr; and many others. As a boy he dreamed of one day leading in such a way that it would make a difference for his generation. He became a teacher, a military officer and combat warrior fighting in Afghanistan, a county commissioner, and is now running for a seat in the Congress of the United States. I was there to help him accomplish his dream.

My point is this: our dreams drive us. But dreams don't just "happen." They are realized by knowing and implementing principles that are non-negotiable. These principles empower our dreams to come true.

It is said that a young boy was found staring out his bedroom window at the moon when his mom came in his bedroom to put him to bed. He turned to his mom and said, "You know, Mom, one day I am going to walk on the moon." Who could have imagined that 32 years later he would step on the moon's surface? James "Jim" Benson Irwin became an aeronautical engineer, test pilot, United States Air Force pilot, and astronaut. He served as pilot for Apollo Lunar Module for Apollo 15. He was the eighth person to walk on the moon.

As Edgar Allen Poe wrote, "Those who dream by day are cognizant of many things that escape those who dream only by night."

T.E. Lawrence once said, "All men dream but not equally. Those who dream by night in the dusty recesses of their minds awake to the day to find it was all vanity. But the dreamers of the day are dangerous men, for the many act out their dreams with open eyes, to make it possible..." James Irwin was that kind of "dangerous man." The best way to make your dreams come true, like his, is to wake up to these principles that empower you to make what might only be fantasy into a tangible, lived reality.

I once asked, "Where can one go from the little village of Providence?" Now, I know. Actually—anywhere. You just need to know where you want to go and how to get there. That's what this book is about—helping you discover, accomplish, and live your dream.

Your dreams are best discovered and realized by what I call the "coach approach." This approach is described in the chapters that follow. Let's begin with more about how this approach has worked in my own life. Then we will see how the coach approach worked well for a business owner and his top directors. The phenomenal success he and his business experienced in a mere eighteen months will underscore the power of the coach approach. Finally, I'll highlight how and why coaching works in relationships, businesses (for-profit and nonprofit), institutions, and ministries. It's an exciting journey!

"Every great dream begins with a dreamer..."

—*Harriet Tubman*

Questions for Personal and Professional Impact
- What were your identifiable dreams during your formative years?
- What were some of the advantages and disadvantages of your childhood experience?
- Have you, or will you, pursue those hopes and dreams?

"The pivotal moments in your life are always made up of smaller pieces, things that seemed insignificant at the time, but in fact brought you to where you need to be."

—*Elizabeth Norris*

The Backstory

INTRODUCTION—PIVOTAL MOMENTS ALONG THE JOURNEY

"Never forget that life can only be nobly inspired and rightly lived if you take it bravely and gallantly, as a splendid adventure in which you are setting out into an unknown country, to face many a danger, to meet many a joy, to find many a comrade, to win and lose many a battle."

—— *Annie Besant*

I am writing from the busy and multicultural Heathrow Airport in London, having a quiet moment of reflection at The Crown Rivers Cafe while waiting on a flight to Edinburgh, Scotland. There was a defining moment in my life that happened years ago, long before I had traveled around the globe to some 30 countries. It occurred in a chemistry class when I was in the eleventh grade. My friend and I were not paying attention when the teacher, Mrs. Woodley, called on me to answer a question about the lab experiment. My heart started pounding and my mind immediately went blank. The seconds ticked by as Mrs. Woodley waited expectantly at the front of the classroom. My friend leaned over and gave me an answer. Yes, the wrong one! When I repeated it, the class laughed. My face flushed and I looked down at my hands in my lap, embarrassed. Mrs. Woodley responded firmly, "Gary, I would like to see you after class." Everyone around me murmured, and I became uncertain and anxious as to what to expect.

The bell rang, the class ended, the students left, and I was alone with Mrs. Woodley. She was known to be one of the school's best teachers, teaching some of the more difficult science courses. A kind but serious sort of teacher who didn't allow any playing around in her classroom. She was seated at her desk as I approached and stood respectfully by her. She kept looking at the notes on her desk, and finally, after a long quiet pause, she stood and placed her right hand on my left shoulder. Her facial expression carried concern yet caring. It seemed she looked into my soul with those steel-blue eyes. She spoke in a challenging but kind and confident tone when she said, "Gary, you can do better than this." That was all she said, but she communicated so much more. That was a defining moment in my life. Why? Because she saw something in me that I didn't see in myself. She believed in me when I had limited belief in myself. She helped me see the best in myself and catch a glimpse of my preferred future. It was, truly, a life-changing moment. I thanked her and left the room. I was grateful for her words of encouragement instead of a lecture or a criticism. I knew something had happened within me. I couldn't articulate it at that moment, but I knew it intrinsically.

I became an excellent student. In time, I earned four degrees. More importantly, I started on a path of personal and professional growth that continues even now as I sit in the Heathrow airport writing about the experience.

Mrs. Woodley didn't realize it then, and neither did I, but what happened in that experience was what I now call the "coach approach" to learning and becoming. At that moment, she gave me a safe place, she instilled confidence in me, she helped me see the potential within me, and she helped me glimpse a dream that would come true. That moment changed my relationship with myself and with her. In the months that followed, she became not only my teacher, but also my coach. Looking back, there were other pivotal moments on my journey.

Believe it or not, as a university student I majored in science. However, during the last couple of years I spent in the science program, I was also involved in ministry, and I began to feel torn between my future career as a dentist and a powerful call to ministry. I struggled with this decision. It was agonizing. Finally, the decision came to a head when I finished my pre-dental work at the university and went in for my final interview with the faculty committee. I knew before the meeting they were going to ask me why I wanted to go into dentistry. I didn't want to lie, but I knew if I were honest with them about what I was wrestling with they wouldn't like the answer. Sure enough, during the interview I was asked, "Mr. Crawford, why do you want to become a dentist?" I responded that I liked people, I thought I would make a good dentist, and the flexible schedule and good income that would come with a career in dentistry would allow me to maximize my time in ministry. It got quiet around the table until my chemistry professor spoke up. He used the metaphor of a violin. What he meant was this: I should pursue my heart—my passion. In that instant another pivotal moment occurred. Interestingly enough, like Mrs. Woodley, it came through another chemistry teacher. That was the moment that helped me cross the line into finally making the decision to abandon my pursuit of a career in dentistry and, instead, follow my calling to the ministry.

When I arrived home and told my wife, Freda, she was not surprised at all. I was grateful for her support. After finishing my biology degree and teaching science for a couple of years, I attended Southwestern Seminary for my master's and doctorate degrees. This involved intensive study in theology, languages, psychology, and counseling. I did this while leading a historic county seat church to make a difference in its community and beyond. Eventually we found ourselves in Gainesville, Florida, where I served 34 years as pastor of Westside Baptist Church. Those years of ministry were filled with growth and global influence. The grace of God and the support of the Westside Church family made it so.

Then came another pivotal moment. Twenty-eight years into our service at Westside, Freda was diagnosed with multiple myeloma. For the next ten years, she fought the disease with courage, faith, and continued ministry contribution. Freda was a science teacher holding a master's degree. She was a musician, a vocalist, and an incredible mother. And yet, in near disbelief, as she battled cancer, she returned to school to earn her PhD and teach as adjunct professor until the disease returned with a vengeance. Two years after her loss, I summed up this experience in my second book, *Grieving: My Pilgrimage of Love*, which helped me process this new phase of life without the wife of my youth. The thesis of this book was that grief can either kill you or make you stronger. We had shared so much—our faith, 39 years of marriage, two children, four grandchildren, education, travel and adventure, teaching, ministry, and of course, abundant love. At first it was difficult to see a way forward without her. I wasn't sure I could stay at Westside after her loss, but through God's grace and the love and support of a wonderful church family I was able to enjoy five more years of leadership. It was a stabilizing time for me with additional growth-years for the church, but still, I sensed that a change was coming, and I began to prepare myself for it.

While I was on a mission trip in the African bush, trying to understand the next steps in my life and develop a new vision for this season, I experienced my next pivotal moment. I took a walk with my Bible and a notepad. By the end of the day I realized the Lord was asking me to move forward by leading the church through a transition which would eventually result in leaving my place of leadership. It would be a three-year transition. When I returned from the trip, I shared the plan with the church leadership, and we proceeded to put it into action; it came to fruition almost to the month, three years later. The transition was an emotional roller coaster of letting go, yet it was also a laboratory for learning multiple leadership lessons.

During that time, as I was learning how to lead in transition, I was in my study when I looked up and saw a book on the shelf that I had purchased some years earlier, *HalfTime*, by Bob Buford. As I reviewed the book, I noticed that I had started reading it sometime earlier but had stopped, which was very unusual for me. I began reading it again, and discovered that it truly "had my number," so to speak. Bob Buford was an entrepreneur and philanthropist who established the Leadership Network and the HalfTime Institute. Buford writes about how moving into the second half of one's life can be a meaningful time for revitalization and establishing a new vision. When I went to the bookstore to purchase a newer edition of *HalfTime*, I discovered he had developed a 27-hour intensive course on transition, "From Success to Significance," in Dallas, Texas, which I eagerly attended. It was in Dallas I learned that their work revolved around the coach approach. I thought I'd always had significance in my life, so that was a bit of a problem for me. It was during this intensive course that I was first introduced to coaching, and as a part of that program I was assigned a talented leadership coach, Bob Durfey, for one year.

I was going through a difficult time; the soil felt unsteady under my feet. Through my work with Bob, I began to see the power of coaching in my own life and the lives of others. I decided to undertake an intensive study of coaching and enrolled in the Professional Christian Coaching Institute (PCCI), where I took "The Essentials of Coaching" and loved it. Then I made a decision to pursue my credentials through the International Coaching Federation (ICF), which is the gold standard for the industry. That started me down the path of professional coaching. I came to understand how coaching could be applied to one's personal life, marriage, family, missions, ministry, and business. Since then I have sought to do just that.

Bob Durfey used the coach approach to help me find my own best answers, because the premise of coaching is that the best answer is within oneself. He helped me look deep inside about my own values, vision, and purpose and, via the coach approach and useful metaphors, he walked with me through a pivotal personal and professional transition. I greatly enjoyed this work and began coaching my own clients while working toward my associate coaching certification. I worked through that academic process for three years, completed the coaching practicum, mentorship, and necessary exams.

During my transition, I realized we are all in a transition of one type or another most of the time. Change is unavoidable, inevitable, and it often presents itself when we're least prepared for it. As difficult as these times might be, however, moments of transition are also rich opportunities for us to experience growth and exploration; they provide pivotal moments for life change.

Coaching and pivotal moments go together. The coach approach helps us go inside ourselves and find our best answers by being willing to ask the right questions, being open and honest, and having a passion for learning the truth about ourselves and about life. It empowers clarity for next steps. Let's look more closely at the meaning and process of the coach approach to life and business.

★ ★ ★

"Neuroscience is teaching us that words hold tremendous power to either ignite positive growth or slow our forward movement. As coaches, we want to pay attention to the words that our clients use and thoughtfully choose our own words as we summarize, reflect, reframe and ask curious questions."

— *Christopher McCluskey*
founder of Professional Christian Coaching Institute

Questions for Personal and Professional Impact
- What are some of the pivotal moments across the years?
- Which pivotal moments in your life changed you and/or your direction?
- What transition are you in now and what have you learned from the past that is helpful now?

"The fastest runner in the world has a coach... The greatest dancers, singers, speakers, and even business executives have coaches. Why? Because coaches help even the best become better."

—Bob Durfey
Captain, Retired U.S. Coast Guard

COACHING DEFINED

"If you want your life to be easy and comfortable...if you want to coast to the finish line, this journey is not for you. But if you have a deep desire to be of use, to learn and grow right until the day you die, you'll find planning an invigorating challenge."

— *Jim Collins*

The International Coaching Federation defines coaching as, "Partnering in a thought-provoking and creative process that inspires people to maximize their personal and professional potential." While some people who are not familiar with coaching may confuse it with therapy or mentoring, there are distinct differences, as outlined below:

COUNSELING—has to do with the past - therapy

CONSULTING—analysis and giving expert advice

MENTORING—provides experience and modeling

DISCIPLESHIP—being with and centering on biblical truth and spiritual growth.

Coaching has to do with the *present* and *preferred* future. The *premise* of coaching is that the best answer is found within the person.

The coach is responsible for the *process* and the person being coached is responsible for the *progress*. A simple model for this is found on the following page.

C - clarify the issues

A - address the obstacles

L - look for creative options

M - move forward

Some of the benefits are:

- A safe place
- Objective feedback
- Built-in accountability for positive outcomes
- A resource for creative ideas
- Greater clarity and renewed energy
- A source of encouragement
- Positive outcomes will be experienced in all key areas of your life

A study of Fortune 1000 companies using coaching showed these percentages of executives reporting benefits:

- Increased productivity by 53 percent
- Increased customer service by 39 percent
- Reduced costs by 23 percent
- Increased profits by 22 percent

Individuals who received coaching saw improvement in:

- Working relationships
- Team-building

- Reduction in conflict
- Business relationships

Good coaches provide support by:
- Helping create and sustain motivation
- Gaining clarity about action plans
- Accountability
- Determining resources
- Dealing positively with decline
- Being open to feedback and how to receive and give it

According to Dr. Nadine Greiner in her 2018 article "Making the Business Case for Executive Coaching," the "demand for executive coaching has experienced rapid growth. All signs indicate that executive coaching is a sound investment. Studies report an impressive ROI of 500-800 percent. The International Coach Federation (ICF) has presented a body of research demonstrating that coaching tends to generate an ROI of between $4 and $8 for every dollar invested," (2019).

"While there are a multitude of different tangible benefits associated with executive coaching, many benefits don't appear as line items on financial statements. A survey reported by Clear Coaching Limited found that executive coaching resulted in improvements in work relationships within a team (50 percent frequency), employees' abilities to see others' perspectives (47 percent), and improved atmosphere (40 percent). In a world where the strength of an organization's culture is increasingly trumping salary levels in terms of importance to employees, these intangible benefits are more relevant than ever.

An often-overlooked intangible benefit of executive coaching is stress reduction. A study by Jan Ramsøy and Sigrid Stover Kjeldsen, in cooperation with the Norwegian University of Life Sciences, found that coaching reduced executives' stress levels by, on average, 18 percent after only eight to ten coaching conversations. Perhaps what's most powerful is the fact that effective coaching appears to be contagious! Research by Dr. Sean O'Connor and Dr. Michael Cavanagh of The University of Sydney found that the closer employees are situated to individuals who have participated in coaching, the higher their levels of well-being.

There's an associated ripple effect. A 2013 study by Anthony Grant found that executives who received coaching experienced effects that transferred over into the executives' family life, including heightened work–life balance and improved relationships with family members. Whether you're examining bottom-line results or the holistic impact on people's lives, executive coaching is a benefit to everyone in and around an organization."

Clearly the case is strong for coaching. No wonder it's an eleven-billion-dollar industry and growing. It adds dollars to the bottom line while simultaneously enriching quality of life.

Coaching is a different way of thinking, based in curiosity and respect for the other person; it's also a different way of relating, in which you're asking instead of telling. You're helping a person process. With a good coach, progress can be unlimited. On the other hand, not every person is coachable; when I meet a new potential client, I have to qualify them to determine whether the coaching relationship will be effective. The sooner that is understood the better; otherwise you're essentially wasting the time of both the coach and coachee. A coachable person has a positive attitude toward growth, change, and becoming. They have a certain amount of humility that allows them to say, "Help me learn and grow." A coachable person is willing to be accountable. A coachable person is willing to enter a trusting relationship and be vulnerable. If those markers are present, the client is most likely to have great outcomes.

If I'm working with a group, the entire team must be qualified. It's possible that not every team member will be coachable. We establish the need for a positive attitude and set expectations. The essential principles of my leadership coaching include vision, clarity, strategy, values, principles, emotional intelligence, team development, tools, and resources. It may be equally said that not every coach is an effective coach. The coach should be qualified as well.

Personal growth is a tangible thing, and the degree to which we remain receptive to continued growth and experiencing life as an adventure determines whether we are truly getting the best out of life. If we don't grow this year, we're simply going to relive the same kind of year over again. We'll continue with the same way of thinking, the same attitudes, the same kind of relationships, and, ultimately, we'll have the same kind of outcomes. Rather than reliving the same year over and over again, we can choose to make a commitment to growing, becoming, and changing by developing a vision and a path toward it.

Coaching is a mirror. If it is to be authentic and genuine, then each time I help someone look into their life, I must also look into my own. I need to constantly look in the mirror as I coach to see what needs coaching in my own life. It's very difficult to separate life coaching and leadership coaching, just like it's difficult to separate the personal and professional. In order to perform successful leadership coaching, to some degree life coaching must be a part of that. First and foremost, I'm a professional leadership coach; I want to develop leaders. I'm also a performance coach. I don't want the client to just have an insight and stop there; if they do, nothing will come of it. I want to see my clients behave and perform in a different way so they can accomplish more. I want to help them identify their dreams and figure out how to pursue and fulfill them. It's very fulfilling to see people make the significant changes necessary to accomplish their goals and then watch those achievements magnify in their lives.

It is my hope that this book will give you, the reader, the tools necessary to make the desired changes in your own life. Only you have the answers you need, and this book will help you ask the right questions to set you on a path toward a deeper sense of fulfillment in both your professional and personal life. I know that if you apply these principles, do the work to look inside yourself and find your own best answers, you will see your dreams come true. Not only that, but as an effective leader you can help others discover and live their dreams well.

★ ★ ★

"You don't build a business, you build people, then people build the business."
— *S. Truett Cathy*

Questions for Personal and Professional Impact
- What is unique about coaching?
- What are the benefits of coaching?
- Why is it important to quality a coaching relationship?

"The Real Learning of anything starts when you begin doing."

—*Christopher McCluckey*
Four of Professional Christian Coaching Institute

The Coaching Process

Leadership Coaching—A Spiritual, Personal, and Professional Approach

"I never cease to be amazed at the power of the coaching process to draw out the skills or talent that was previously hidden within an individual, and which invariably finds a way to solve a problem previously thought unsolvable."
— *John Russell, Managing Director, Harley-Davidson Europe Ltd.*

I n future chapters we're going to hear directly from the team of directors at Chick-fil-A on Archer Road, about how leadership coaching and the coach approach enabled them all to experience transformational personal and professional growth. First, however, I'm going to give you an overview of how I structure the coaching process; coaching is about more than having conversations and asking questions. It's about developing a clear vision for your future, carefully assessing where you are today, setting goals, and creating a solid plan for achievement. Coaching is a journey of self-discovery, and it's a journey I will lead you on, starting right now. It won't always be easy, but it will be worth it.

As the coach, it is my responsibility to maintain complete confidentiality and remain within my competencies. During our sessions, I make sure we're clear about the topic on which we're working and do good timekeeping. As the coach/coachee relationship develops, I establish trust by creating a safe and supportive environment and demonstrating respect. When I need to broach a sensitive topic or ask a deeply personal question, I ask the coachee for permission first. It's imperative that I remain present during our time together but am non-directive and avoid asking "why" questions. Effective communication is critical; I participate through active listening and try to avoid interrupting the coachee. I help them explore their thoughts and feelings, without expressing judgment. I ask open-ended questions and summarize a coachee's answer back to them to be sure I've understood their meaning correctly. I use metaphors and analogies to help them understand their situation, and when appropriate I refer them to other resources, such as books or Scripture passages I think they would find helpful. I don't present myself as the person with all the answers, as the essence of coaching is for the coachee to find the answers within themselves.

A leader is someone who has a clarified vision; a high relationship quotient; a personal growth plan; an understanding of business finances; and the ability to execute with excellence. This is what we're moving toward, developing these qualities. Take some time to think about leaders who you have admired throughout your life, both from afar and in your own experience. When we reflect on effective leaders, we often leap to the well-known people with incredible legacies, like Martin Luther King, Jr. or Winston Churchill. But great leaders don't always work on such a large scale. The memorable teacher who had a lasting impact on your young mind, the baseball coach who showed you the value of diligence and teamwork, the boss who took you under her wing and became both friend and mentor—these are the leaders who touch our lives in a way we may not appreciate until years later. When you remember the leaders who have shaped your life, what are the qualities they possessed that made them so valuable? What is it about them that you continue to admire after all this time? Keep these qualities in mind as you develop your goals and strategies.

?
Coaching
Questions

Working in tandem with my coachee, I facilitate their positive outcomes and results by creating awareness. I ask questions that allow the coachee to examine their life in an objective way and encourage them to identify their values. I help them differentiate between facts and interpretation and identify the disparity between choices and values. Coaching, of course, isn't just about talking, it's about action; part of our work together includes designing an action plan to ensure further forward momentum. Sticking to that plan, meeting goals and hitting milestones, requires me to promote self-discipline and accountability in the coachee, and evaluate their progress based on the timeline established.

During my coaching work with the Archer Road Chick-fil-A team, we incorporated faith and spirituality into the process. We acknowledged that this is a faith-based company; from its founding, it has been based on principles of the Christian faith. As we moved through leadership principles, business principles, psychological principles, and relational principles, we would often raise the question of, how does Scripture enlighten or speak to this issue? How is the Holy Spirit leading you through this principle? Some of the directors wanted recommendations for particular Scripture passages they should read, and I would give them suggestions. Gradually, the directors began engaging Scriptures in a very personal way, and they would return to me after their initial reading for a deeper conversation. They would ask more questions: What does this passage mean? What does it say? What does it mean for me *today*? How does it apply to my life, purpose, vision, mission, goals, and responsibilities? Some of the best impromptu discussions we have had come from this enterprise. Often, I will begin the team coaching sessions with a passage from Scripture, and now they do that at their directors' meetings as well. As they experienced this spiritual growth, they would share their experience of what the Lord was doing in their life and what they were seeing that they hadn't seen before. Their own personal testimony became a powerful expression of growth.

? Coaching Questions

The challenge in coaching this group was to help everyone become the persons they wanted to be and, in so doing, develop the organizational principles that would move the business forward. While some of the directors were more hesitant about the coaching process than others, they all came to recognize that this was an opportunity for them to grow both personally and professionally. We started with discussions about identity, vision, strategy, and principles that empower people, and eventually led into policies and procedures, which built strong management. When there is alignment between personal and professional values, that's when you have your best outcomes. Coaching is believing the person has the best answer within themselves, so it's my job to manage the process while the person is managing the progress. Accountability is built into a good coaching relationship.

Let's break down the structure of the coaching process a little further. There are three major components:

- Clarify
- Simplify
- Amplify

Each of these is broken down further into smaller, more manageable pieces, but let's first define how each one works.

Clarify

To clarify is to take a long look at who and where you are, make an honest assessment of your strengths and shortcomings, and determine the core values in your heart and your vision for the future. It's about articulating your vision to gain trust and compel action. You're making a decision here to do the hard work and make changes that will bear fruit for you and your business down the road. Make a list of your core values, a moral compass of what you believe, to use as a compass for the standard of behavior you expect and for decision making. What are the defining principles of your life? A principle is a fundamental truth. You're also defining your present reality and establishing your hopes. Take a look at your business: what are your numbers, your sales and profits, and what would you like them to be? Create a purpose statement for yourself—what guides you? Why do you exist?

Simplify

To simplify is to streamline all those thoughts, hopes, and dreams, working through them until you've established a clear vision for your desired future. You're setting a direction with specific goals and outcomes. Create a vision statement—what inspires you? What does your preferred future look like? With a vision statement, the focus is on tomorrow. With that established, the next step is to write a mission statement. Your mission statement should sum up what drives you, what you do and for whom, and how you do it. Your mission statement will be the basis for developing strategies. A strategic plan is a personal or corporate plan that will maximize opportunity, growth, accomplishment, and fulfillment. A set of SMART goals will be the guide for developing the strategic plan. As you assess your objectives and goals, keep in mind the difference between these two things.

Amplify

Amplify is about measuring your achievements and paying them forward. Which outcomes have you met? What charts, graphs, and testimonies speak best to what you've accomplished? How has your attitude changed? Are you experiencing greater focus and heightened energy? When you can successfully model leadership for your own team, you can begin the process of leadership duplication; by using what you've learned through the coaching process, you can coach others and create a coaching culture where everyone benefits and grows. Having this coaching culture in your organization means increased honesty and trust; leadership development; motivation; change management; retention; stronger vendor and customer relationships; and personal and team growth. Developing a coaching culture is not a simple task. It requires a clear vision, strategy, strong senior leadership, team commitment, communication, and behavior changes. The rewards for this hard work, however, are endless.

The outline on the next page provides an at-a-glance overview of the steps described above:

CLARIFY

Decide
Inside story—What's your dream?
Core values—Who are you?
Clear vision—Where are you going?

Reality Defined
The value—What's at stake?
The weaknesses—What is hindering your dream?
The numbers—What do they tell you?
The hopes—What is your preferred future?

SIMPLIFY

Engage
Clear vision—What's the outcome?
Compelling mission—What do you do?
Strategy—How will you do this?
Trust—What's the one nonnegotiable?

Aim
SMART goals—What's your structure?

AMPLIFY

Measure
What is your attitude?
Do you have increasing energy?
Are you reaching your goals?
Are you duplicating leadership?
Are you creating a coaching culture?
Living my dream—Am I doing it?

As you can see, the coaching process is expressed by the acrositc D.R.E.A.M. This is the process that enables the discovery and accomplishment of dreams.

In the time I've been coaching Ray's team of directors, we've accomplished a great deal. We've established trust, something the group struggled with before our work together started. They've learned how to hold one another accountable, without it being taken personally. Their meetings have been streamlined in order to be more effective in less time. At these meetings, they set action items, so everyone walks out the door knowing what their responsibilities are in the days to come, and they follow up on that, tracking one another's action items and making sure everyone sticks to the plan. Together they work toward common goals and don't compete within their areas of focus.

They've seen real results in the business. Their sales have gone up over 30 percent each month since their move to the new location, and they've broken several hourly, daily, and monthly sales records; this profitability has allowed them to implement a new incentive plan.

While my coaching work has only been with Ray and the other directors, a significant part of the coach approach is teaching the coachee to replicate their own success by coaching others to find their own best answers using the same methods. The directors of Chick-fil-A at Archer Road created a number of materials that have allowed them to grow leadership among their employees, even for those who are not involved in our sessions. They've put together an operational manual that explains their vision, mission, and values; establishes setting goals; creates a structure for the work environment; and they have clear job descriptions and operating systems for all the positions and responsibilities at the restaurant. In addition to providing these valuable tools, they've put into action a Leadership Development Plan for team members, called "Foundations of Flagship," that has been extremely effective in developing leadership skills among participating employees.

If you're a manager or director looking to develop your team but are unsure of how to move forward, then let's look at how the following signs of a healthy, thriving team culture can help; the way they helped Ray and his team at Archer Road.

Seven Signs of a Healthy Team Culture

- A clear purpose: Purpose reveals what you believe and determines why you do what you believe.
- A clear vision: Vision pictures outcomes and must be cast every day.
- A set of clear values: Every organization operates by a set of values. They must be identified, aligned, and repeated.
- A commitment to collaboration: A failure to collaborate results in the "silo effect" and the loss of synergy.
- A high level of trust: Trust is based on transparency and commitment to do what you say, how you say, when you say.

- A commitment to growth: This requires a resolve to "lean into discomfort" for the purpose of constant improvement.
- A habit of celebration: We multiply what we celebrate.

How many of the above can you honestly say apply to your team? This exercise should give you a starting point, at the very least; an idea of what you're hoping to work toward in the future. Just as you as an individual can sit down and create your vision statement and mission statement, these things can and should be done for an organization as well. Your strategy for developing this culture will first require understanding and commitment from senior leadership, without these individuals on board, you will struggle to engage other members of the team. Ideally, creating a healthy team and coaching culture will actually involve engaging a professional coach to train the team in coaching practices. Even without a professional, however, there are a number of actions you can take to develop leadership and synergy among your team.

Implementing a Healthy Team Culture at Your Organization

When you're ready to start this important work, it's crucial to ensure that everyone feels as though they have a voice and their contributions to the process matter. If you approach this process with excitement and a positive attitude, you'll communicate to your employees that this is more than just another meeting. Gather your team and have them brainstorm with you on casting your vision for the organization. Communicate the strategy for attaining that vision, while encouraging collaboration and engagement. If you can foster a sense of ownership in every team member, they will work with you toward these goals, no matter what their position in the organization. If you teach coaching skills to your staff, they can engage one another in coaching, which will improve communication and make their workplace interactions more meaningful and effective. This can't, however, just be an exercise everyone tries once at a staff outing. It requires a long-term commitment to coaching routines. Develop a method for assessment and continually evaluate the program.

As an example of a vision statement, Ray's team states their vision as:

"To provide our guests and our team with a five-star experience by excelling in every part of the business and strengthening the Chick-fil-A brand everywhere, to the point that our guests, CFA corporate, and other CFA stores want to visit and see what we're doing."

It's a vision statement because it's aspirational while still being attainable. In comparison, their mission statement is:

"A culture of unity, collaborating together with the same end in mind, excelling at the highest level in: remarkable service, craveable food, blazing speed, bulls-eye accuracy, hospital cleanliness, increasing sales, growing profit, and consistent development of people."

That is what they are doing, every day. Any employee can use those statements as a frame of reference when they need to make a decision or assess whether something aligns with the store's values and mission. They clarify expectations for everyone who works there, serving as a guide and a model for excellence, and ensure every single team member—from the owner to the directors, to the managers and employees—is on the same page. They provide a clear directive in terms of what everyone is working toward on a daily basis. Aligning company values in this way might only be the first step of many in the journey toward greatness, but it is a step that paid off mightily over time.

★ ★ ★

"As coaches, we equip people to be in touch with their best selves."
—*Clyde Lowstuter*

Questions for Personal and Professional Impact
- What are the three major components of the coaching process and what do they mean?
- Why is confidentiality essential?
- What does create awareness mean?

"Too many of us are not living our dreams because we are living our fears..."

— *Les Brown*

Meet the Unique Company

"To glorify God by being a faithful steward of all that is entrusted to us and to have a positive influence on all that come into contact with Chick-fil-A."
— *Chick-fil-A Corporate Purpose Statement*

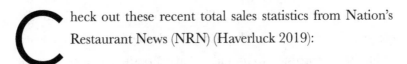

Check out these recent total sales statistics from Nation's Restaurant News (NRN) (Haverluck 2019):

1) McDonalds with 38.52 billion
2) Starbucks at 20.49 billion
3) Chick-fil-A jumped from 7th to 3rd with 10.46 billion
4) Subway
5) Taco Bell
6) Burger King
7) Wendy's

What makes these numbers even more impressive is the fact that Chick-fil-A only operates 2,548 restaurants in 47 states as well as Washington D.C. as of 1/19/20 (Taylor 2019). The only states remaining without a CFA franchise are Alaska, Vermont, and Hawaii. This is less than one-sixth as many as the top three earning restaurants and less than half as many as the rest of the franchises ahead of it. Unlike its competitors, the Chick franchises are closed one day per week—every Sunday. That's a total of 52 non-operating days, not counting holidays. As a result, lost sales are estimated as nearly $1 billion a year (Taylor 2019). Why would they close each Sunday when they could make another $1 billion a year? It doesn't seem to make good business sense—or does it?

How does such success happen? What is the driving factor? The answer is simple. A commitment to excellence rooted in the founder's values, which still drives all major company decisions.

It's no secret that the founder of Chick-fil-A, S. Truett Cathy, was a committed Christian. The "corporate purpose" on the company's website reads, "To glorify God by being a faithful steward of all that is entrusted to us and to have a positive influence on all who come into contact with Chick-fil-A." There is no surprise then, that Cathy's policy stemmed from his religious beliefs (Miner 2016).

In his book *Eat More Chikin: Inspire More People* (2002) Cathy said, "My brother Ben and I closed our first restaurant on the first Sunday after we opened in 1946, and my children have committed to closing our restaurants on Sundays long after I'm gone. I believe God honors our decision and sets before us unexpected opportunities to do greater work for Him because of our loyalty."

It is generally understood that Cathy's practice of closing on Sunday stems from a conviction in his faith. From the early days of his first restaurant, the Dwarf Grill, he decided he would close on Sundays. He felt it was giving honor to the "Lord's Day" and honoring the spiritual life of employees, as well as their families, by having a day of worship, rest, and restoration. This is still the company's practice today. This conviction has remained so steadfast that the CFA franchise located in the Mercedes Benz Stadium even remained closed during the 2019 Super Bowl game, disregarding a potentially enormous opportunity for sales. This was clearly a noteworthy statement. "Excellence" then, is not defined by profits, but by a faith that provides foundational values. This faith influences policies that bring integrity to business practices and care for employees, family, and community.

This also means that every employee has a guaranteed day off, every week. This certainly helps the company during the recruiting process, and makes for a healthier environment on and off the job. It promotes excellence. As retired clinical psychologist Jan Fite stated, "Treating Sunday as a day of rest has always been relevant. We all need to step out of our everyday lives and disconnect from routine, make time for ourselves and loved ones, and get out of performance mode. Especially today, when we are subjected to the constant onslaught of news and social media." This practice promotes work-family balance and contributes to the well-being of the business and employees (Miner 2016).

Excellence in serving the community is another mainstay principle of CFA's business practices. As Karen Miner shared in her article, "The Real Reason Chick-fil-A Is Closed on Sunday," CFA franchise owner Carmenza Moreno operates the CFA restaurant just three blocks from the Dallas Cowboys' stadium. Since the restaurant is closed on Sundays, she chose to make a decision vastly different from her competitors. Moreno "decided that rather than barricade her restaurant's parking lot every Sunday, she'd open it up to allow fans to park (and pay). But the money doesn't pad Moreno's pocketbook—it all goes to the groups who man the lot each Sunday. In four years, the parking lot fundraiser has generated more than $62,000 for local organizations." CFA is involved in their local communities in multiple ways, making a contribution to a stronger community life. Such thinking is a mark of excellence (Miner 2016).

Is Chick-fil-A always closed on Sundays, no matter what? Not exactly. There have been specific reasons through the years that have prompted CFA to open its kitchens to meet the critical needs of the community. These include serving meals in the aftermath of Hurricane Florence in 2018, feeding "stranded passengers at Hartsfield-Jackson Atlanta International Airport in 2017, feeding first responders of the Orlando Pulse nightclub shooting in 2016, and providing support to first responders and victims in 2015 after storms and tornadoes slammed Dallas." This kind of community contribution is, again, a mark of excellence. Even though this doesn't make commonly understood "good business sense," which says losing one day of business a week will put any company at a serious disadvantage, biblical wisdom has proven otherwise (Miner 2016).

"Despite being open for 14 percent fewer days a year than competitors, Chick-fil-A is dominating the fast-food industry," says *Business Insider*'s Kate Taylor (2019). "While Cathy's original reason may have been based purely on his Christian faith, analysts say that the decision to close on Sunday is also a brilliant business decision."

It's noteworthy that before S. Truett Cathy passed away, "he created a contract that stipulated the company remain private. His heirs can sell the chain, but it must remain private." Why make a decision that could cost his heirs billions? "Cathy knew that publicly, Chick-fil-A could not be as charitable as it is privately." The man of faith and conviction believed in charity as much as he believed in his charitable decision to close one day a week. This is an act of excellence in legacy thinking and will continue to bring good things to each generation (Vigliotti 2019). In addition to the Sunday closing having numerous benefits for employees, businesses, and communities, there are two other driving factors for the success of this unique company.

One is service. The service is exceptional. As Khalilah Cooper, CFA's Director of Service and Hospitality, shares, "It doesn't matter if the guest is pulling through the drive-thru, ordering for delivery, picking up curbside, or dining in the restaurants, the company's goal is to provide best-in-class performance for every single experience. Each of our occasions, we want our customers to think of Chick-fil-A as a place that they can go and they know they're going to be taken care of, they know it's going to be fast but that the food will be great, the service will be efficient, and they will have genuine hospitality and a team member who is there to take care of them." Cooper says, "Even just those small moments, regardless of what channels our customers choose to engage with us, can really make the difference in a day," (Oches 2019).

Chick-fil-A uses a customer experience model that allows the customer to provide feedback on everything from the temperature of the coffee to the cleanliness of the dining room. The OSAT "the overall satisfaction" matrix measures seven primary components that define excellence. They believe that their most dissatisfied customers are their *greatest* source of learning. The exceptional service that comes from constant feedback and constant training enables Chick-fil-A to outpace most others in quality service.

The other driving factor of Chick-fil-A's success is just good food. The menu is simple and the quality is consistent. The sales prove the point—excellence. It is also in their progressive menu planning. The CFA kitchen is always looking for recipe improvements like the gluten-free bun, the removal of high fructose syrup and dyes, use of sea salt, cage-free eggs, and non-antibiotic chicken. CFA continually tries new items like the chick-n-sliders.

"In May 2019, it was revealed that the company is exploring the idea of adding some vegan options to its chicken-heavy menu. While there are a few vegetarian-friendly items currently available, and customers have the option to order chicken-less salads and wraps, veggie-loving visitors to the fast food chain have generally been left out in regard to vegan entrees. But Chick-fil-A's executive menu director Amanda Norris told *Business Insider* that the company is currently conducting research into offering a 'vegetarian option or a vegan option,'" (Vigliotti 2019).

It's worthwhile to know, as stated on the CFA website, "S. Truett Cathy always maintained that he wasn't in the chicken business, but the people business. From knowing his customers by name to forming lifelong friendships with his employees, Cathy viewed his business as more than a source of revenue for him and his family; it was a source of encouragement to others" (Chick-Fil-A.com, 2019).

Chick-fil-A is a unique company. Unique in origin, unique in growth, unique in policy, and unique in success.

Chick-fil-A is a dream come true. The dream of S. Truett Cathy, a man of faith. A faith that birthed the vision and values that gave direction to a mission. The dream continues to come true through his legacy of leadership, and encouraging others to dream too. I know. I have worked with Chick-fil-A Archer Road's owner and directors for two years. I have heard their dreams, seen many of them come true personally and professionally, and others are still in the making! This is the exciting story—their story—told in this book.

No wonder Chick-fil-A's motto is "It's my pleasure."

"We change the world, and ourselves, by our response to unexpected opportunities."
— *S. Truett Cathy*

Questions for Personal and Professional Impact
- What was the dream that gave birth to Chick-fil-A?
- What is unique about the company?
- What about this company is relevant to your life and career?

"Before you are a leader, success is all about growing yourself. When you become a leader, success is all about growing others."

— *Jack Welch*

MEET THE COURAGEOUS TEAM

"The true price of leadership is to place the needs of others before your own. Great leaders truly care about those they are privileged to lead and understand that the true cost of the leadership comes at the expense of self-interest."

— *Simon Sinek*

Before we move forward with learning more about the team coaching process, let's meet the team. They are an incredible group of hardworking, dedicated people with a wide range of backgrounds, gifts, and skill sets. When I met them the first time, I immediately recognized the potential in the room. I was excited!

Ray Holloway is the owner-operator of Chick-fil-A, Archer Road, Gainesville, Florida, and has been for over twenty years. He's a sharp businessman who carries a certain posture of intensity. The thing I most appreciate about Ray is how he cares for his people. His leadership and support of me as the team's coach made the defining difference.

Over the years Ray would meet once or twice a year with other operators to discuss the challenges and responsibilities of the business. Ray raised the question, "How do you create self-sufficient leaders?" One operator said the best thing he had done was to hire a coach. Ray took that to heart and soon began to look for an executive coach. He discovered my business by searching the internet and coming across my website. He recognized my previous leadership in ministry and concluded this would be a win-win in that "Gary could handle the executive coaching and offer a level of spiritual coaching that many in the field don't offer."

When we met, I explained that as a leadership and performance coach I was committed to seeing change. He indicated he was ready for both personal and professional growth; I recognized his sincerity and perceived he meant what he said. We put a coaching agreement in place and set a date to meet the team.

Ryan Summers is the Executive Director. He is 24 years old and in his seventh year working for the company. He started working at CFA at seventeen while a student. Having had the opportunity to work at four different CFA locations over the years, it has given him the advantage of a broader understanding of operations. His goal is to be an owner-operator by age 30; he wants to have the same positive impact on others as he has experienced within the CFA organization. Ryan is already well on his way. He is mature for his age, has an incredible work ethic, and is very focused in his leadership.

Misty Emerson is the Talent and Development Director. She finds, recruits, on-boards, and trains staff. She is gifted and persistent. A native Floridian, she and her husband have two children. Her 21-year old son has cerebral palsy and requires full-time care. She is fully devoted to seeing that his every need is met. I have met him, and he is a delightful young man. Misty spent nine years in church planting and revitalization. She is also the co-chair of a nonprofit organization in Haiti. When Ray invited her to join CFA, she was hesitant at first. But after numerous conversation, she agreed, saying, "It was a God-inspired decision." When Misty feels called to something, she is "all in." Gotta love that.

Laura Wisener is the Director of Sales and Brand Growth. Laura covers all marketing functions encompassing sales, events, fundraising, and community visibility. She, too, is a native Floridian. She and her husband have two beautiful daughters. Before becoming a part of the team, she was a gymnast coaching competitive gymnastics. Knowing many of the local residents, Laura made an immediate contribution to the business. Laura has a tender heart and strong commitment to the business and the community.

James Lincoln directs the "heart of the business"—the kitchen, where the food is prepared with measured excellence. When I began working with the team, he had been with Chick-fil-A for ten years. Originally from Tallahassee, he is now a student at the University of Florida and "bleeds orange and blue." A hard worker, he enjoyed the feeling he got from "having a hand in making something great." He said, "You can't take the material stuff with you when you leave this life, but in succeeding in my goals, it makes me feel like I'm fulfilling my purpose."

Joe Wendling was Drive-Thru Director when we first started coaching. Although originally from Maryland, he graduated from the University of Florida as an engineering major and carried the Dean's list. He started with the company in 2013. He is now moving into the Leadership Development Program with a goal of becoming an owner. He is on a certain path to do so.

TJ Graham is the Facilities Director. Another native Floridian, he and his wife have two children. Having a background in construction, he began work at Chick-fil-A in 2001. With his experience and cooperative spirit, he makes a contribution across the whole of the business. TJ is the kind of guy who will make you feel at home.

As you can see, the team members bring a kaleidoscope of personalities, perspectives, attitudes, talents, and skills to the table, each making their own particular contribution. They also bring their own challenges in making the team, a team!

Our first meeting surfaced the need for growth in trust, positive attitudes, confidence, clear direction, organizational policies and procedures, time management, and creating a coaching culture.

My rather daunting task was to provide the level of coaching that would enable personal, professional, and organizational growth—all at the same time. In addition, the owner had several large goals; to relocate the business, increase annual sales by $2 million, develop improved organizational policies and procedures, create a leadership development program for the employees, and initiate a coaching culture within the business. The relocation was to happen in nine months and the $2 million increase in sales in the twelve months following. Yes—you read it right!

You will learn about the amazing outcomes in the pages that follow.

As Christopher Reeve noted, "So many dreams at first seem improbable. And then when we summon the will, they soon become inevitable."

Now that we know the players, let's look at the playbook.

★ ★ ★

"It takes courage to grow up and become who you really are."

—*E.E. Cummings*

Questions for Personal and Professional Impact
- What observations can you make about the team and how do they apply to your circumstance?
- What were some of the challenges of the team?
- What were the objectives of coaching?

"Culture is simply a shared way of doing something with passion."

—Brian Chesky

PART ONE

CLARIFY

1

DECIDE

"There are few things more powerful than a life lived with passion and clarity."
— *Erwin McManus*

This section will take on the first of three pivotal principles from my coaching philosophy: Clarify. This meant articulating the team's vision to gain trust and compel action. The first part of clarification is to *decide*—making a commitment to change and determining where the work needs to begin. Decision empowers forward movement. Before we could begin truly moving forward, there was a certain amount of diagnostic work that had to be done in terms of identifying the most problematic core issues so we could develop a method to address them. That is, we needed to look at the inside-story. As the team began their work with me, they discovered just how deep the challenges they faced were before they could fully function as a highly effective team. A lack of trust, for example, was mentioned again and again during the interviews. Establishing this core problem was a crucial first step in moving forward.

One of the initial aspects of being an owner-operator that appealed to Ray was the culture. He saw it as an opportunity to be in business for himself while also having a partner. Chick-fil-A serves in true partnership with their owner-operators. This allowed Ray the flexibility he needed with his family; he could attend his kids' school activities and be there when they needed him, provided he did the work whenever necessary. That, in addition to being able to work with people—something he's always enjoyed—was a big part of the appeal. Typically the store's employees are younger. When Ray first started he was closer to them in age; he was 26 and they were roughly eighteen to twenty-one. Now, at 50, he has a bit more spread, but working with the people, the flexible schedule, the partnership and the culture have kept him motivated and engaged as an owner-operator.

Ray has been the owner-operator of other CFA stores, but he's willingly relinquished the keys when it was time to move on to a different location. Most owner-operators have just one location, although some have two and there are a few with as many as three. Ray's goal is to have a second store in Gainesville. Attaining the level of excellence necessary to get approval for that second store was part of the motivation behind bringing in a leadership coach; Ray wanted to grow leaders and give his employees the opportunity to improve themselves. He didn't realize, however, that before that could happen the directors would need to grapple with the lack of trust I heard about many times in my early meetings with the team.

According to Ryan, the team was disjointed, operating in separate fragments that didn't cohere as a whole. "We didn't trust each other. It was hard," he said. "It made work really hard, because some of us would try and take on too much and then not ask for help." Not trusting other team members to execute was a large problem. "They would commit to doing it but it would never get done. So that was the biggest issue."

Another issue Ryan spoke about was that individual team members were more interested in their own personal gain and growth than group gain or core restaurant growth. Ryan is not the only director who would like to have his own restaurant one day, and team members with that particular goal were focused on "what we could do as individuals to grow and be ready to leave, rather than set up [CFA Archer Road] for success."

Other members of the team were unsure about engaging in the coaching process. Laura is very open about the fact that she was hesitant to do it. "I was the one on the fence," she said. She was nervous and didn't know what to expect; she had experience being a coach but wasn't sure how it would feel being on the other end. "I kind of knew, well, okay, he's going to talk me through these things or he's going to push me in a direction that I may or may not want to go in. So I was a little apprehensive, but as we continued it was of course better than I thought it would be." Fortunately she discovered her fears were unfounded. "I knew what coaching was from being a coach, but it's different. I'm coaching gymnastics, he's coaching life, and it's just different."

When I began working with the team of directors, they were all in different places. Gainesville being a college town, many of the employees are in that age group, but some had much more experience, both in life and in the workforce. As Laura said, "There were three of us that were, let's just call us much more mature. You know, a little older. Two out of three of us had been here a long time. We were your 'lifers,' as we referred to ourselves in the group. We were more set in ourselves and where we were. The others were charging, you know, young guns. They're on their way up the ladder. 'I'm going to do what I need to do to make myself successful.' We all had different outlooks. We had different outlooks on what the business needed, on what the business had, or what its potential was, or why we were doing what we were doing."

Of the personal and professional issues the team faced, Laura also agrees that the biggest problem was trust—because there wasn't any. People had different agendas and were not on the same path. "We weren't pushing in the same direction." As the marketing person, Laura stands somewhat outside of the operations; at the time, Misty was still fairly new but she was working on getting the culture going in a different direction with the new hires. "She and I have the people part of the business, if you will." Then, of course, there are the other issues surrounding the kitchen, the drive-through, and the operations of the restaurant itself. "It's all one business but our job descriptions are very different." It was frustrating to feel as though the team members didn't understand how their colleagues contributed. "I have to explain what I do a lot. What options there are for marketing are very different today than they were five years ago, ten years ago, sixteen years ago when I started. So that job description has changed probably fivefold. I have no doubt it's changed more than any of the others, just because of the internet, social media, every camera and tiny computer. Everybody can reach you at any given time, for better or for worse."

The focus of Laura's work is driving sales. "It could be increasing the number of families that come in for family night; that might not be on the radar of whoever is managing the front of the restaurant. And they're like, 'Oh, she's bringing in more people. Now I've got more people to deal with.' Or, 'Oh gosh, what is she giving away today?' Because I used to give the store away a lot." To promote CFA Archer Road, Laura used to bring samples to other businesses; that required going to the kitchen and saying she needed a certain number of nugget trays by a certain time. "I had to really think about, okay, what is this store going through right now? Is it lunchtime? Because if it is, it's probably not a good time to ask for some nugget trays. I thought about that, but not everybody understood why I needed what I needed when I needed it. Because there was not a lot of communication."

Laura feels it was the focus on character that brought about the most remarkable outcomes. "Once we got to a point where we agreed to trust one another, once we got that, everything else was okay."

TJ wasn't necessarily for or against professional leadership coaching. He looked at it as a learning opportunity since it was new to him. "I was feeling several things, some anxiety, nervousness, and most importantly, excitement. I knew we would talk about aspects of my personal life as well as my work life. For me, what was different was once I got past all of those feelings, it was time to put in some work."

Some of the highlights for TJ were learning about things "that I personally had never thought about. Purpose statement, vision statement, and a mission statement. I think I knew I had direction, goals, and a purpose, but what exactly that meant in a structured plan was going to be revealed before my eyes. It was different because it not only helped me learn things about myself but also people I interact with, both on a personal and professional level. It also helped me build trust in myself and with our director team. We had to learn to trust ourselves before we could learn to trust others."

Another issue TJ identifies as holding back the group during that time was a lack of chemistry. "As we began to earn trust within ourselves, it helped with our chemistry, not just individually but with the team. Communication was also an issue. If I can't trust whether I say that I'm going to do something, and if I don't commit to it and complete it, then how is someone else going to trust what I say?"

Joe had "no clue what to expect, honestly," when it came to the coaching process. "I'm like, all right, it's a leadership coach. I'm guessing he's going to try and dive into the way that I lead people, maybe change my leadership style." Having never met or spoken to anybody who had ever worked with a leadership coach, Joe had no frame of reference by which to gauge his expectations. Joe set any doubts aside and went in with an open mind. "Okay, we're doing this," he said. "Let's do it!"

As with the other directors, the lack of trust was an issue for Joe. "We didn't trust each other because there would always be snickering behind each other's backs," he said. "I would go talk to this person about this guy or they would be talking to this person about me. Sometimes this person will go talk to that person, you know. I just didn't know how little we trusted one another. There was a lot of pot stirring."

As the group began to develop that newfound trust, Joe recalled that one of its main benefits was "knowing that we were all working in each other's best interests. I know that 'trust' is a very broad term. For us it meant trusting that everybody was actually going to do what they say, when they say, how they say. That was the first key foundational thing that we had to get over. And we were able to do that. I wouldn't say it happened quickly. It took some growing pains. We would all be sitting around the table and Gary would put the spotlight on us, and we'd have to talk about our issues and learn how to speak into each other's lives."

Joe also makes a direct connection between this lack of trust and the business itself. This issue facing the director team held them back, keeping them from pushing forward to the highest level of production they could potentially achieve. "Our productivity was the biggest business-related thing hampered by that," he said. "A lot of times we were so worried about this person or that person, what they're thinking, what they're doing. So we weren't able to work to our full potential because we were always worried."

Before the coaching process began, Misty felt "a misalignment with what we were doing and where we were going." She also observed some character issues that had to be dealt with, "some super steep character issues. Personally I would say that was the challenge facing the team. And then a lack of understanding of what we were doing." She makes the analogy of getting in your car and driving because you need to get somewhere, but not knowing where you're going or how you're going to get there. "So basically we were all just driving around in circles because that was what we were supposed to be doing. Professionally I think our team suffered because of that." Misty recognizes that the problems were not necessarily limited to the director team but extended to the team of employees working under them. Without proper leadership models, they had no strong example to follow. "Businesswise, they were seeing one thing from our director team but hearing another thing from us, so we were all hearing and seeing different things. There was a definite lack of trust because there was no foundation to anything being said, no backup to what was being said. It was all just empty words."

Going into the coaching process, Ray didn't fully understand the scope of the personal issues. "I knew we just had a lot of truth that we needed to go through," he said. "I knew that we needed to just kind of gel better together, but I thought we were pretty good. When we started coaching, I understood that we had some issues and so we started with foundational trust. Using a scale of one to five, I was thinking that my team and I had a trust level of a solid four, but later found that it was more like a two. We definitely discovered that we had some issues once coaching started."

Ray is talking about an exercise I had the team do, where I had them write down on an index card, anonymously, the level of trust each director had in their team members on a scale of one to five. Ray expected the team had at least a level-four amount of trust in one another and was deeply disappointed to learn that it was only a level two. That revelation, however, gave us a better understanding of where we were starting from and what work ultimately needed to be done.

"It was a process that Gary put us through," Ray said. "We talked a lot about trust. We agreed to be able to talk into each other's lives. To do it without taking offense to it or taking it personally. We submitted the index cards and then Gary revealed where we stood. So it was a great exercise, but it only worked because Gary was able to make us feel confident and comfortable that we could share this information and that we would be able to deal with it without letting it become heated. It was handled very, very well. Once we were through that we started the trust building exercises he had for us."

Understanding that the trust level was not as it was first perceived around the table, I had the team ask themselves and one another, 'What is it that you don't trust and why?' So the first part of the process was determining what the issues were that were contributing to the trust issue. I led the directors through understanding the benefits of building trust and the continued deterioration that occurs when trust is absent. As Ray recalled, "One of the main trust issues was the failure to follow through. Some team members weren't following through on things they agreed to do for others. So Gary had given us this phrase that I went and put on the wall, 'Do what you say, when you say, how you say.' That seemed to resonate with us pretty well, because one of the key issues is that we would say we were going to do something for someone and then not do it. That would break down our trust in one another."

When Ray says he put that phrase "on that wall," he's referring to the fact he literally had "Do what you say, when you say, how you say" painted on the wall of the conference room. The point—trust action, not words. This motto has become the perfect distillation of what the directors have come to expect from one another, and what has enabled them to have the well-earned trust that exists between them today. At any given moment, a team member can ask themselves, "Am I doing what I said I would do, when I said I would, how I said I would?" and if the answer is anything but a wholehearted yes, they have the opportunity to correct themselves before they interfere with that trust they've all worked so hard for. If I say to you, I'm going to do something, I'll tell you when I'm going to do it, and if I follow through on that with integrity, then that integrity is congruent with values. Once it became apparent that it was a foundational building block, then we could build trust.

Ray just wanted to help the team elevate where they were. Some of his leaders were on the younger side, just out of college, and they needed some additional, professional help in learning how to think and be more strategic. He realizes now he was asking them to do things without being very diligent about showing them or telling them how. "So I brought in someone who could help me do that more intentionally, as my time was very divided with some other things. Building leaders is important to me, yet I wasn't focusing. This helped make it all work out and refocused me to get to where my purpose is, and then the results come from that. They just needed that additional support."

On the other hand, I also made sure that the coaching process would work with everybody on a personal level, with anything they have going on in their world. I didn't want it to only work with the team in their professional lives, because if they need something personally, if that's on their mind, they'll have difficulty focusing on work-related items they need to focus on for the sake of the business. So we have to have that balance there. As I continued working with the directors on an individual level, I also focused on building trust between us, so they would feel comfortable sharing their personal issues with me, someone who had been a stranger until recently. It's not necessarily an easy leap to make, but we built those relationships and I became a trusted confidante in addition to a coach.

Having clarified the core needs and desires of the team, we were ready to move to the next step of clearly defining their present reality.

★ ★ ★

"Adhering to a daily schedule that is led by your vision and run by your priorities is the surest path to personal freedom."

—Mark Ford

Questions for Personal and Professional Impact
- What were some of the issues that needed to be clarified?
- What was the most important and influential issue?
- What was the primary objective of the owner?

"To be of value, values must be rooted in revealed transcendent moral truth."

— *Gary Crawford*

2

REALITY DEFINED

Core Values and Clear Vision

"It's not hard to make decisions when you know what your values are."

— *Roy Disney*

B y helping the team establish their core values and clear vision, through leadership coaching I began to lead the group forward by evaluating their hopes and weaknesses. Learning to articulate their desired accomplishments played an important role in the team's work. The next step to "clarify" is "reality defined," which means establishing a deep understanding of the current situation. What was working? What were some of the existing successes? What challenges lay ahead? Getting a sense of each director—their position and responsibilities, as well as personality and management style—would also bring into focus for me how to best draw from their strengths and help them overcome their weaknesses.

After Ray brought me in to work with the team as a leadership coach, I started at once by working with the team as a whole and with each individual seperately. In this way, personal and team growth were happening simultaneously and at a similar pace. This model is essential in accomplishing the desired relationships and performance. When I first met with the team there was some apprehension, some uncertainty as to what coaching really was, and also some anticipation because they were sincerely wanting to see change.

At that first meeting, we set the agenda for what our meetings would look like going forward. I communicated my confidence and belief in them, and we celebrated some of the good things that were already happening with the business. We spent some time identifying patterns they were experiencing: feelings of being overwhelmed, lack of clarity, desire for more self-awareness, need for prioritizing and decision making tools, and doubting their abilities to make the necessary changes. We talked about financial matters and I clarified their top expectations.

In dialogue the directors were able to identify some of their feelings pretty readily; to assist them with this I would ask prompting questions that led them to reflect personally and as a team. As their coach, it was my job to diagnose, so to speak, how they were functioning as a team and where the company was as an organization. As Ray mentioned in the previous chapter, one of the store's challenges is its location in a college town. While this can be a benefit in terms of the sheer number of potential employees, in practice it can be difficult when it comes to training and depending on young people primarily occupied with their studies, not to mention the constant influx and outflux of such a transient demographic. The students are constantly arriving and departing, graduating, going home for the holidays and such.

Ray agreed that finding potential leaders in this group can be a challenge. "It's definitely a mind shift because going through college, it's just getting a job to earn money in order to make ends meet. They don't necessarily take the job opportunity seriously. Being in the industry that we're in, it's very hard for people to look at this as a career opportunity versus just a stepping stone or something to do until they can get something else. It's very hard to get people to think in that way, that this is a multimillion-dollar business. Currently we have 140 employees, and we're shooting for 185. We're a big operation."

It's not an exaggeration. Of all the stores currently operating in the five states of the southeast region, Chick-fil-A on Archer Road is the third-busiest. "We're a pretty big deal as far as sales," Ray said. This made it imperative to get the team to start thinking about business; it was key that they all come to understand they are part of a multimillion-dollar operation with dozens of employees and responsibilities, not only to their customers but to their fellow team members. It was time for everyone to start thinking strategically, not just about their own positions but about growing the business as a whole, with Ray's ultimate goal of opening a second store in mind.

"This could be a career for you if you choose it, whether it's a career at this CFA or becoming an operator on your own," Ray said. "I've had two employees that have become operators, and I have another one currently on the team who is trying to become a future operator. So we're working through those processes and trying to generate those opportunities to help everyone achieve what they want to achieve, whatever that may be."

One of the principles that became a major focus of our coaching work together was character; we also emphasized integrity. "For me they go hand in hand," Ray said, "and we really focused on making sure that we kept ourselves at high character." This went for existing employees and also extended to hiring practices. "We can teach you how to do what we do, but we can't necessarily teach you character. You already bring that to the table, especially at the age where we're hiring a lot of people, between seventeen and twenty-one." By then a lot of what makes a person who they are has already been set in place. "It's hard to change. It can be done, but it takes a lot of time. So character and integrity, that's what we focused on. And I would say that was probably a game changer for us moving forward."

Making character a central focus of CFA Archer Road's business practices meant instituting a drug-free policy, even though the restaurant is located in a college town. By holding all employees to this high standard, Ray made it clear to both current team members and potential job-seekers that a certain level of character is considered a prerequisite for any position there. It has helped them to maintain a positive culture. They've lost several employees as a result, but as they've seen the morale and the culture of the store improve, there is no doubt that it's been a net-positive for everyone. This was a bold and risky move for the store, to create a hardline drug-free policy in a town where most of their potential employees are young college students. However, it did a lot to establish their expectations to current and potential team members of all levels, and to foster that culture of character and integrity.

"There are a lot of great, great kids out there," Ray said. "Some of them choose to do the thing that we're saying we're not going to allow them to do, and then there are other kids that say, I don't want to be around people who are doing that. So we were having this divide of, 'We don't want to be in your workplace because of the choices these other folks are making.' By establishing and enforcing a drug-free policy, it has created a healthier culture. We doubled down and I've lost some good people, but if I hadn't made those terminations I would have had character issues of my own. When the team saw me doing that, I think it really sunk in that this was for real, and this is what we're going to do."

As a result of setting this policy and following through, the rest of the team feels like they can trust Ray and trust his character. They know that he cares for them, and now "we have a fantastic relationship around the table. We're more than just colleagues, if you will. We're family. That's how we feel about each other."

The directors foster this feeling by doing "life check-ins" ⚛ during their team meetings. They talk to one another about what's going on in their lives, about their children, about their faith and spirituality. "We go to a different level," said Ray. "We don't just talk about work."

As new policies and procedures were being put into effect at the store, and as "Do what you say, how you say, when you say," was gaining momentum as a motto of sorts, another idea was taking shape in terms of the store's ultimate vision. The team's vision is to provide the guests—and employees—with a five-star experience by excelling in every area of the business, and strengthening the Chick-fil-A brand everywhere, to the point where guests, corporate, and other stores look to CFA Archer Road as a leader. Once the directors were able to articulate and summarize this vision, they were able to distill it into one catchword: flagship.

"We want to be where everyone wants to go," Ray said. "The store everybody wants to mimic. Which is a lofty goal, but why not go for all of it, right? Why not strive for the top? That's our vision, to be that leader, that example, and that's how we came up with 'flagship.'" In addition to this vision, Ray and the team were also able to set concrete goals for 2019, designated as flagship goals, including reaching $9 million in sales, a $2 million increase from the previous year.

As the directors made progress establishing trust, laying out their core values, and setting goals, I was also using the coach approach with them as individuals to tap into their leadership potential. Ryan's understanding of the coach approach was that it could help him become a problem solver rather than a problem creator, or someone who would rather just complain about a situation without endeavoring to improve it. He was learning to lead with questions that would bring in others' abilities and hopefully lead them to a better quality of life, not just in the workplace. In addition to asking questions to provide self-reflection or self-assurance, he began to see how it could be practically applied in a restaurant environment to help people learn and achieve greater proficiency and competency.

Using the coach approach, we worked on Ryan's communication as well. "I think definitely the first step was not being directive or leading out of power," he said. "Together we read the book *The Servant,* where the story reveals the way a leader can lead with power or lead with authority. I always thought I led with authority because I worked really hard alongside my coworkers, but through coaching I realized maybe it wasn't always that way. Maybe I did have some directive or power-driven tendencies. I was invested, and when people let me down, I would immediately revert back to those tendencies."

Now, when Ryan is faced with something difficult or when people let him down, he leans toward the coach approach and asks questions, helping them to find and apply helpful insights. He no longer shies away from communication, as he once did when we started coaching. Instead, he is at the point where he and Ray can say, "We're going to go have this talk right now," and they can get the other person into the office and have the conversation. Now he doesn't shy away from that at all.

As an aspiring owner-operator himself, Ryan has gained a great deal of insight into the intricacies of Ray's position, such as the fast pace and quick maneuvering from one area of the business to another. The owner has to be able to pivot from looking at the front line and serving the guests, to assessing the product and ensuring its quality meets their high standards. From there, the owner has to move to the back of the house, checking the kitchen for cleanliness, and then into the office to respond to emails and pay bills. Even when the "work" day is over, Ryan noted, "you go right out the door to your home office, where you're focusing on personal growth. So being in a position where not only Ray's doing that but I'm doing that, the information that's going through my mind never stops. So if I'm not sharing that with anyone, my mind is full all of the time. My list of things I want to get done constantly gets longer, on both a personal and professional level. It's important to get away from just doing what's urgent and communicating with others, like, 'Hey, can you take care of this while I do something that's important for the business?'"

Misty, having never played sports or been coached in any other arena, approached the process with the mind of a psychology major, thinking it would be more like counseling. I assured her this wasn't the case, but without a frame of reference, she just couldn't imagine anything else. Now, she understands the difference between coaching and counseling. "We're not talking about things and working them out, we're making decisions and growing and putting feet to those decisions." The initial coaching sessions were hard for Misty, emotionally. "I have a very hard time articulating what I feel or what I know. Sometimes I get really stuck in a place, and Gary was always very graceful in helping me dig myself out of that. He never ever picked up the shovel and started digging for me, which I now know to be a foundational element of coaching. Some days I felt like I just couldn't dig myself out of that hole until we actually got there, and I didn't realize we were already there. It was a lot of hard work but it was very productive."

Misty continues to work on trust: trusting herself, trusting others, and trusting God. That's frequently the end result of our coaching sessions, posing the question, "Are you trusting God with this?" Despite being an admitted worrier and, to some extent, a people pleaser, Misty nevertheless refuses to compromise what she believes in order to please others. Even when she does the hard things, she still carries the weight of what she knows people will feel about her as a result. "I want to be liked and I want people to view me as successful, so those are the things we worked on the most, personally," she said. Professionally Misty has worked hard on how to alleviate some of the stressors in her life, because her instinct is to say yes to everything. "But then you've got to have time for everything, so scheduling and calendaring have been huge for me."

According to Misty, truth was the principle that brought about the most remarkable outcomes. "Finding our own truth was huge, and standing on our own truth was huge. Allowing permission for others to speak truth into our lives and receiving that permission back. We were all feeling a great sense of tension, frustration, anger, and angst with one another. And we were trying to run a business at the same time. Very few of us were doing what we say, when we say, how we say. Even if you identified a problem and created a solution, you could not believe that was going to be executed or communicated or followed through on, so it felt like a whole lot of time wasted. It was very frustrating."

As the directors continued to emphasize character and integrity, Laura noticed a drastic change, particularly as Misty did the hiring. With previous directors in that position, Laura had observed the emphasis was more on practical issues like, "Can you work these hours? Great, you're hired." As changes began taking shape, new hires came under greater scrutiny in terms of their character. "And when that character piece comes into play," Laura said, "you've already taken care of the other issues that are going to come four weeks down the road. You know, 'Oh, sorry, I can't work that day anymore.' Or, 'Oh, I'm sorry, I know I told you I could, but that was just so you would give me the job.' There's so many different things, but the character piece is so important because that lends to the rest."

Laura recalled that in addition to the group meetings, individual meetings, and homework assignments, there was a lot of soul searching to do. As the team developed their mission and vision statements, they also spent a great deal of time clarifying essential aspects of themselves, the core values that define who they are. Aligning their actions with those values, once established, became an important part of their work. "It was the steps. It was, okay, now that you know what your vision is, what your mission is, who you have said you are, this is who I think I am. So if this is who I am, and I'm that on Sunday with my family, and then I'm that Monday through Friday with work and I'm that Saturday at the kid's birthday party, that's who I am. And I think that's part of what helped us to find that glue, if you will."

Laura agreed that the group learned to trust one another by living out their new motto, "Do what you say, when you say, how you say." Also of great importance was striving for excellence daily by serving one another. Part of her personal vision is to serve others well by nurturing them. As a business, that's part of the five-star experience the team speaks about providing for their guests. By caring for one another, they can better care for the guests. If Laura were to create a graphic to tell the story of how coaching has changed them, she said, "it would be simple, just an arrow pointing up, because it's just a constant, we're looking up all the time. If we're looking where we should go first, then as we're continuing this climb toward flagship, it's an upward movement. Sometimes it might stop, it might pause, but it's consistently going up."

Joe has also experienced significant growth in his leadership style through coaching. "I don't know if anybody would call me the Energizer Bunny of the restaurant; but I'm always moving around fast. I always like to push people. I don't like to do it all. I like to jump in when I need to, but I also like to give people the chance to do it themselves." When the restaurant breaks records for volume, it makes him proud, and even if he's not present when that happens, he's thrilled, because that means he's prepared the people who work for him to succeed whether he's there or not. "If we break a drive-thru record for most car counts—most cars served at the drive-thru per hour, most sales per hour—I am more satisfied when it's my team that accomplishes this. It's like that old saying, you know how good a parent you are by how good your grandkids are. I like seeing the team that I helped train, training others to do all of this."

Joe is the first to admit, however, that his leadership and delegation skills have come a long way. When he first became a team member, he wanted to see his name on the wall as "employee of the month"; he put a lot of value on those kinds of accolades. The shift may have started even before we began our work together, as he was already getting older and maturing, but he still possessed what he considers a self-centered leadership style. For him, the biggest shift he can attribute to leadership coaching is this growth in how he behaves as a manager and supervisor. "Before I was just doing what I needed to do. I wasn't concerned about the personal growth of others."

What surprised Joe the most about leadership coaching was that "we didn't really address leadership-related skills right off the bat, because the first thing we worked on was building trust. I then realized this would be helpful." Over time, as the focal point of our meetings shifted, Joe saw the changes bringing about remarkable outcomes. There was a significant impact on relationships, the organization's strength, and profit outcomes. A lot of this grew out of asking questions about why they were here and what they wanted to accomplish. "That started with us personally and then developing that 'why' for the business with a purpose, with a mission, and with a vision. Because when we started this, Ray knew why he wanted us to work with a leadership coach, but we didn't have anything past that. We first needed to answer the questions, 'Why are we doing this? Why are we all here? What are we all working for?' If I were to sum it all up, the purpose would be that one principle, to clarify purpose, mission, and vision."

As part of his inspiration, Joe referenced basketball coach Jim Valvano when he accepted an award from ESPN back in the nineties. Valvano had been diagnosed with brain cancer, and he tragically passed away not long after receiving the award. During his acceptance speech for the Arthur Ashe award, he said, "How do you get from where you are to where you want to be?" It was a question that had a huge impact on Joe. "That's something that just rang in my head when we were developing the purpose, vision, and mission statements. It was such a powerful speech. If we want to set the vision and mission, we have to visualize the way there. So our restaurant was able to develop a vision, which in one word, is flagship."

TJ also worked to define the opportunity and needs in his area of responsibility, which as Facilities Director, supports all the other team members. He defined reality clearly when he said, "The issue before us is performance, and that will improve as we improve ourselves."

By asking themselves the important questions—'Why are we here? Why are we doing this? What are we working for?'—the team successfully developed their purpose, mission, and vision, and established where they were going. Now everyone who works at CFA Archer Road knows what they're all striving for, and they can all sum it up in a single word—flagship

(See Appendix I for Organizational Structure.)

★ ★ ★

"Simplicity is the ultimate sophistication."

— *Leonardo da Vinci*

Questions for Personal and Professional Impact
- What are "values" and how are they related to character?
- How do values determine policy and procedure?
- How does the principle "Do what you say, when you say and how you say" relate to values and integrity?

PART TWO

SIMPLIFY

"Employee engagement is the emotional commitment an employee has to the organization and its goals."

—Kevin Kruze

3

ENGAGE

"The ability to simplify means to eliminate the unnecessary so that the necessary may speak."

— *Hans Hofmann*

The next primary principle of this coaching strategy, *simplify*, means to set a clear direction with specific goals and outcomes. Now that the group had a concise summation of their desired vision—"flagship"—our focus turned to building strategies for moving toward it. Establishing trust became the centerpiece for achieving their ultimate goal. "Do what you say, how you say, when you say" became a fundamental principle of the team.

The first essential step of "simplify" is "engage." This requires not only developing a clear vision for the business and a picture of the preferred outcome, but creating tangible and intangible representations of that outcome—the former being tools like mission statements, the latter being a stronger sense of trust. Together, all these strategies empower the team to reach their goals.

When I talked with the directors about their initial expectations, I learned that they wanted to see some attitude changes; namely, they wanted to see increased positivity. They wanted to be able to count on one another in a more confident way—do what you say, when you say, how you say—and they wanted to see a culture of honor. They also wanted to see employees take pride in their professional appearance, and they wanted to have clear goals to work towards. Those were some of their initial top expectations.

In order to get them there, I gave them a number of tools to work with. One principle we developed was the idea that when you fight for your limitations, guess what? You get them. What you tolerate, you will have. To keep striving for greatness, we took a common tool, the "3 Cs of Hiring"—culture, capacity, and craft—and drilled down more deeply until we had come up with our "**7 Cs**"—character, chemistry, conviction, competence, consistency, catalyst, and called, with "called" meaning a real sense of ownership of the job. We built these into the leadership development plan, a compilation of our policies, procedures, job descriptions and more. As we moved through the coaching process, the directors were able to successfully model these for the team members working under them, and they began to see positive results.

There were a number of issues with scheduling and time management. Each of the directors carries a lot on their plate; some of them have families that require their attention, some are still in school and are balancing work with their studies. As a result, I knew that all the directors would benefit from working on calendar management and setting priorities that come from their vision and values. We talked a great deal about learning how to give **"your best yes,"** and the **"yes/no principle."** Essentially, when ☀️ you say yes to something, you're effectively saying no to something else. Whatever else you might have been able to participate in or accomplish during that time is now off the table—whether it's dinner with your family or a study group or just some time you had hoped to set aside for yourself. So when you make a commitment, ask yourself first what you will now have to give up in order to fulfill that commitment. Then make your decision based on your vision for yourself and the values you're trying to prioritize.

We talked about the importance of starting your day well, the principle of **"win your morning, win your day."** When you ☀️ wake up every day, ask yourself, "What am I excited about today?" and then make an effort of nailing that. The team has made a real effort in terms of forward planning. By Thursday of each week they have completed their schedules for the following week. And in less detail, the month, quarter, semiannual, and year. This allows them to plan ahead, which minimizes stress and scheduling anxiety.

One calendaring principle that I shared has been helpful to me over the years in my own personal struggles with time management, whether it's personal life, marriage, or family. It's important to **plan** ☀️ **something special** for the week, every week, even if it's just a special meal at home. Then plan something a little bit more special for each month, something even more special for the quarter, something else that's even more special twice a year, and once a year to have *the* special thing for a given year. That way you always have something you're looking forward to; something to anticipate and take your mind off the struggles you're experiencing.

Once each director had developed a list of the strengths that were identified, we engaged the book *StrengthsFinder* and the strengths survey. During our monthly meeting we would focus on relating and working from our strengths, which has been extremely important, especially since the relocation. Using questions like 'What *can* I do? What *should* I do? What *will* I do?' has been very significant in helping the team sort out their priorities. Even asking yourself this one simple question every day—'What's the one thing that, if I can accomplish it today, I can go to bed feeling good about achieving?'—can make an impact on how you feel about whether or not you're moving forward toward your goals.

?
Coaching
Questions

Ryan has been instrumental in creating the leadership development plan currently being used to train future leaders for the store. "We call it the '**Foundations of Flagship**' course. Not only is it a Chick-fil-A leadership course that will give people tools to succeed within the company, but it will serve in any venture they want. Our high-school and college employees may not necessarily want to work for Chick-fil-A forever, but we want to give everyone the tools to be successful. To learn how to be a coach, how to schedule their time, what SMART goals are, and to set up their personal and professional growth plans. That part is important because the coach approach has now extended past the group of directors and is now being applied throughout the company. Others are experiencing it as well, whereas before we would have never thought we could coach."

The leadership development plan came from Ryan and I working together to create something tangible to offer employees that would encourage strong talent to stay with the store. "Chick-fil-A already offers scholarships for students, a great work environment, and really good food, but how do we go beyond that? Some employees leave for things we may not offer, so the leadership development plan is something I thought would separate us and demonstrate, 'We're invested in you. This is what we want to do.'"

That was Ryan's first thought for the course. His second was the desire to provide employees with the tools to be leaders in anything they choose. "When I started at Chick-fil-A, I did not think it was going to be my career. I believe this course could be a real benefit to someone taking a gap year from school or looking to build their future. One of the young ladies that just completed the course wants to move to Korea and teach English. She's finishing school and won't be moving for another three years. Now she's seeing Chick-fil-A as an opportunity where people are investing in her, and her growth makes her want to stay with us rather than exploring something else."

While that was the original rationale for starting the plan, the outcomes have demonstrated even further why it's necessary and productive. "We've had meetings with business consultants to see if we can potentially own another restaurant, which would be really big for us. It's currently in the development stage. Ray and I brought to the table one of our emerging leaders, Brianna, who just took the course with us, and we asked, 'Brianna, do you know our company's vision?' She knew the answer right away. She's worked with us for less than six months, but seeing the potential in her, investing in her, and allowing her to grow makes her say, 'I'm going to quit my other job and work with you guys.'"

Another young man working at the restaurant had a habit of apologizing for everything. Even when he didn't need to apologize for anything, he did so out of habit. Ryan observed a real positive change in this person that came from working in a supportive coach approach environment that encourages student employees to become strong, independent leaders.

"Each of us is so different, right?" Ryan said. "So our journeys are going to be very different." When asked to sum up the core message in one sentence, Ryan actually listed a series of powerful statements: "The hard work is worth the effort. Growth is not easy. How to grow personally and professionally. The power of coaching. Fear is a liar. Perspective determines outcome. How the impossible becomes possible." He sees the team's story as one that can inspire fortitude and serve as a model for success. "It's about integrity, congruence. The objective is to align personal and professional organization values."

The coach approach has altered how Ryan interacts with the team members he is hoping to inspire. "It's changed the morale a lot because when we come in now and see something going on that isn't necessarily flagship worthy, instead of going over there and saying to someone, 'Hey, you know, you didn't do that right,' or saying something negative, we ask, 'Tell me what's going on over here? How did you come to that decision?' It's a whole different approach. Now instead of feeling like I just came down on him, my employee feels like I trained them and encouraged them. Often people don't have the 'why.' Coaching really helps bring out the 'why' behind the 'what,' to understand what is right, and what is wrong. It's getting a better result with a better approach; we're correcting something, but we're doing it way differently. So to me, that has changed the morale of the business, because now people understand that they're learning, they're being taught, they're being coached."

Despite Laura's original hesitation about coaching, it's now clear to her that it could not have begun at a better time. "Gary caught me at a point where I was stagnant. A point where I'd had so many people come and go, and it was one of those turning point moments. In marketing, like with anything else, we have this group of people for about four years, and that's a long time. If you have them that long, you're feeling blessed. They start in their freshman year and I say, 'Great, come do marketing with me,' and I train them, show them the things I want them to do. And then they leave. And sometimes they all leave at the same time. That's where I was when Gary walked in. I was frustrated."

Over time, Laura saw how one of the principles we had discussed in our sessions—**what you tolerate, you will have**—was playing out in her life. "I learned that I was a little impatient and maybe a little stubborn and set in my ways a bit. I needed to say to myself, 'Okay, stop. You can do this, move on.' I was trying to keep up with the times and learn how to use social media effectively. I'd hired the right people before. So I learned a few things about, 'What should I do at this moment?' In other words, stop having your little pity party and move on, and start praying about what you want, because you have what you tolerate. So I was putting out what I don't tolerate, and I had to get past myself and start again. What I discovered was that I had all the tools, but I didn't have them where other people could access them."

This is when Laura discovered the value of taking all the institutional knowledge she'd acquired throughout her years as CFA Archer Road's marketing point person, and putting those policies and procedures down on paper where they can be accessed by fellow employees and new hires. Now she has an up to date procedures manual that she can refer employees to when they have questions. That also helped her learn how to coach—she knew how to coach gymnastics, so she knew she had to get those basic steps down before moving to the next level. It's the same with life in general. Those procedures need to be in place for a reason. Procedures for marketing may not be the same as procedures for making chicken in the kitchen, but they still have to be clear, concise, and accessible.

For Misty, the challenges of the coaching process have been fruitful. However, for those about to embark on a similar journey, she does not want them to underestimate the hard work required. What Misty wants people to know is that it's hard, but doing the work is easier than staying where you are and fighting the battles that you're fighting. "It's worth it to unapologetically chase the vision, even if you don't know what the vision is," she said. They didn't have a clear vision at first; they had to create it. "We've created everything since working with Gary. I don't want it to seem like it was just five steps to getting where we are now. We had to learn how to successfully navigate rough waters and find our sea legs."

Misty made the excellent point that the term "sea legs" actually has two meanings. When you first step onto a ship and sail out to sea, you have to find your sea legs onboard and learn how to move around while the ocean passes by beneath you. "That's what it feels like we've been doing," she said. The other definition of sea legs is finding your footing again when the journey is over and you step back onto shore, but it still feels as though the ground is moving under your feet, even when you're standing still. She compared this to one of the challenges the directors have all faced, which is how to work with excellence but still keep up with their families and other responsibilities. So these are the dual challenges they've had to master—working in a fast-paced environment and executing with excellence, and then being able to go home and be present, and recognize that things are no longer moving around you. "When I looked up sea legs, I saw that it has those two different definitions— figuring out how to stand still on a rocking boat, and then when you step off, understanding that you're not moving anymore, you're standing still. I laughed out loud when I read that, because that's what we do."

★ ★ ★

"There's a difference between interest and commitment."

—Ken Blanchard

Questions for Personal and Professional Impact

- What does simplify mean in the context of the coaching process?
- What are several principles of the simplify process?
- How does simplifying lead to a leadership growth plan?

"People who regularly write down their goals earn nine times as much over their lifetimes as the people who don't, and yet 80 percent of Americans say they don't have goals. sixteen percent have goals but don't write them down. Less than 4 percent write their goals, and less than 1 percent actually review them on an ongoing basis. Guess which 1 percent?"

— *Dave Kohl, Professor of Virginia Tech*

4

AIM

Set SMART Goals

"Give me a stock clerk with a goal, and I will give you a man who will make history. Give me a man without a goal, and I will give you a stock clerk."

— *J.C. Penney*

In teaching the team the power of setting SMART goals, or goals that are specific, measurable, achievable, relevant, and time-bound, I used leadership coaching techniques to work with the directors as they executed the enormous challenge of changing locations and bringing their business to new heights. Before entering our discussion of how the team used these tools to further their personal and professional development, let's take a closer look at what SMART goals are and how they work.

SMART goals are one of the most powerful tools available to us. Goals help us define our purpose; consider the time you set aside for reaching these goals as time invested, rather than time spent. Establishing a set of clear goals will give you direction and help develop your strategy for moving forward. SMART goals often prove more attainable because they provide you with a path toward success. SMART goals are:

- **S**pecific—Clear and concise
- **M**easurable—Success is easily defined
- **A**ction-oriented—Within your control
- **R**ealistic—Attainable
- **T**ime-bound—A deadline

You can set these goals for any area in your life, whether your goal is to lose weight, improve your feeling of job satisfaction, deepen your connection with your spouse, or be more engaged in your faith. For instance, if you find yourself glaring unhappily into dressing room mirrors or daydreaming at your desk when you're supposed to be reviewing spreadsheets, you may already have a vague sense of your own unhappiness. Or how about when you're looking at your partner across the dinner table while listlessly pushing the food around your plate, unsure of how to begin a difficult conversation about strengthening your relationship. Or it could be consistently failing to set aside time for prayer and worship, even though every week you tell yourself that this week will be different—you may already know that something has to change. The question of how to implement that change, however, is often a thorny one.

Goals must be specific; otherwise they risk being meaningless. You may say you want to lose weight, but who doesn't? Set a clear and concise goal of how much you want to lose and by when. If you want to feel closer to your spouse, what does that mean—more time spent together, more honest conversations? Be specific.

Goals must be measurable. Otherwise, how will you know when you've succeeded? Create this definition of success before you start, and you'll have something to work toward. Some goals are more easily defined than others. If you want to quit smoking, you'll certainly know whether you've done it. It's a binary; you're either still smoking or you're not. How will you know when you feel more engaged with your faith? Create a scale for yourself—your current level of satisfaction in this area of your life is, for example, only a two on a scale from one to five; you want to be at a four. Some things are easier to measure than others, but with a little thought and ingenuity you can develop a metric for just about anything.

Your goals must be action-oriented, or you'll be incredibly frustrated. If your goal is for your children to be better behaved and always take their baths without complaint, you are likely to be disappointed. If your goal is to enforce stronger boundaries, however—setting a sleep schedule or getting your children to sleep in their beds, not in yours—that's a different story. If your desired goal is greater job satisfaction but your current position is an unfulfilling one, is your time best invested developing strategies to feel more engaged where you are, or would that time be better invested looking for another job? You can't control how other people behave, but you can control how you respond. So if you want to improve a difficult relationship, you can still set goals that focus on reacting differently, drawing from your own set of values.

An unrealistic goal will do you very little good. If you want to lose weight, is it more realistic to try to shimmy back into the jeans you wore in high school, or shed ten pounds over a series of months? Don't set yourself up for failure. If your goal is to start running three times a week, don't expect to be signing up for a marathon in six months. You can still set your sights on running farther and faster over time. Set attainable goals while still pushing yourself to go beyond your comfort zone; achieving your goals should be a challenge, it shouldn't be impossible.

Finally, SMART goals are time-bound. Setting a deadline means on that date you can look back on all you've accomplished and experience a genuine sense of satisfaction, knowing that you're closer to living out your vision. Even if you miss the mark somewhat—you've lost eight pounds instead of ten, or you're only engaged at work 50 percent of the time—you've done the hard work of realigning your time and energy to better suit your values. You can start again, setting another SMART goal and continuing on your journey.

When setting a SMART goal, begin by establishing where you are currently in relationship to your desired outcome. State this in the positive, in the present tense, and with clarity. "On January 1st, I weigh 150 pounds." "On January 1st, I only feel engaged at work about 25 percent of the time." State your desired goal, as aligned with your vision and values. "By June 1st, I will weigh 140 pounds." "By June 1st, I will feel engaged at work 75 percent of the time."

State why each goal is important to you. "Losing ten pounds is important to me because I want to have more energy." "Job satisfaction is important to me because I want to feel like I'm making a difference at my company." If you're setting multiple goals, first place them in order of importance as indicated by the time you currently allocate to each one. Then rank them again, this time in order of their importance to you as indicated by your vision and values. Right here you'll get your first clue as to how to begin restructuring your life; if you've ranked your desire to be more engaged with your faith as your top goal, but you currently spend only one or two hours a week in prayer or study, you'll know immediately that the first order of business is to align your goals and values.

There are, of course, only a limited number of hours in every day, and days in the week, so an important part of finding time to work toward these goals is developing a criteria for "**saying no.**" The team of directors from Chick-fil-A Archer Road speak of this frequently, one of the most valuable tools they gained from our coaching work together was learning how to develop their "best yes." When you say "yes" to one thing, you are saying "no" to something else. Look at your average week, how your time is spent. What are you saying "yes" to that doesn't align with your values? Develop a criteria for "no" based on that.

Maybe you don't know where to start. Maybe you're not sure what goals to set. If you are still stumped and having trouble creating a proper vision, try envisioning yourself at a work celebration one year from now and ask the following questions:

- What have I achieved?
- What will I value the most? What am I most proud of?

- What would I most want said about myself?
- What would I be most disappointed about if not said?
- How have I changed?
- What contribution have I made to others?

With that in mind, continue this personal assessment by asking yourself these questions:

- What is my greatest strength?
- What are my top three priorities for the next quarter?

- What three decisions are causing the greatest stress in my life?
- Where am I stuck?
- What should I stop doing?
- What should I reschedule?
- What do I need to delegate? (What am I doing that someone else can do 80 percent as well as I can do it?)
- What are the three things I can do in the next 90 days that will make the most difference in accomplishing my priorities?
- What are the top three habits I need to develop now?
- If I could only do three things before I die, what would I most want to do?

As I worked with the team on building trust and creating strategies for executing their goals, we continually returned to the idea that it was important for them to share with others what they were learning. That meant around the table with the other directors as well as with the other employees at the organization. We had gone back to the basics—like when Coach Lombardi held up the football to his team and said, "This is a football." Building trust requires going back to the basics, and it doesn't happen overnight. I was open with the team from the beginning that it takes time; you build trust by doing the right things at the right time, by doing what you say, how you say, when you say. Building trust requires taking an emotional risk, and that in itself requires emotional transparency, admission, and forgiveness. Trust must be built from the **other person's perspective**; you gain it by giving that person what they need, not by giving them what you imagine you would need if you were in their situation. This goes back to our working definition of love, which is based on what's in the best interest of the other person. When you're trying to build trust—or rebuild trust—your starting point cannot be your own perspective. You must nurture any burgeoning trust by envisioning this other person's point of view, using what you know about them and also using your words to ask them, What is it *you* need to create trust between us?

?
Coaching
Questions

I spoke with the directors about this idea of having a trust account, where you make a deposit by keeping commitments, and you make withdrawals by failing to keep commitments. You nurture trust by having clear expectations. You build trust by having an attitude of serving one another. We talked about the benefits of trust, and I used an illustration of polarized sunglasses. If you're looking down at the water you can't see anything, but then you put on polarized sunglasses, and if the fish are close enough to the surface of the water, you can see them. Trust enables you to see what you can't see otherwise, the exciting possibilities in the life of the other person and the team with whom you're working. I asked them to read *The Speed of Trust*. This book really imprinted on them that 'trust' is the one thing that changes everything.

My impression of the directors was that they each had significant potential; there was a sense of loyalty that was already there, they had a good work ethic and they wanted to learn. We used a tool that I call the "**confessional approach**"; that begins with owning one's own perspectives and feelings. The approach is for one person to speak to another using statements that begin, "When this happens, I feel..." So it's a confessional statement detailing someone's response to a particular event, circumstance, or behavior, which allows trust to be built by taking away the attack approach and being less accusatory.

Another exercise we started doing early on, which we have used consistently during our individual meetings is called the "**inside story**." If I ask you how your day is going and I tell you something about the activity of my day, but I fail to reveal much about how I processed, experienced, or what I took away from it, then the interaction hasn't deepened our understanding or connection at all. So the inside story becomes very valuable in communication and building relationships. It considers things like: positive feelings about myself and the circumstances, negative feelings, my most frequent concerns, what I really want, etc.

Another tool is "**carefronting**." That term came from author David Augsburger; the premise is that confrontation is difficult and not desirable for most people, but if you care enough to confront, and confront in a caring way, it opens up opportunities for growth. That's a powerful concept. Conflict is inevitable; it's going to occur whenever you have a group of different personalities working together. Any team striving to accomplish a common goal is going to have its challenges, and the objective should not be to avoid these entirely, but to embrace them as opportunities for growth and change.

One principle I believe the directors found extremely powerful was, **"think like a leader all the time**." A leader sees before anyone else, and typically further than anyone else. If you walk into a room, you've got to look and see what others wouldn't see first, and you've got to see the implications before anyone else. This was important for our team as they were learning how to model leadership for others in the business.

We also worked on a model of teaching that we summed up as **"show a person**." Let's say an employee is learning a new task. The ultimate goal is for the employee to be able to perform this task on their own, but first you need to teach them how to do it. We broke this down into a series of steps. First, show the person. You perform the task from start to finish as they watch you. Next, you guide the person as they try, answering their questions and assisting as necessary. Finally, the person does the task entirely, and you offer affirmation, and if there's further training needed you do that as well. So it's show, guide, try, affirm, this principle of teaching what you learn as you move along.

Each of these tools fed into the coach approach process over the following months. During this time we were also preparing for the greater challenge of moving the restaurant to the new location. Of course this was an enormous task, and it was rather intense before the relocation. Because they wanted to have a "flagship" relocation, we set goals to guide them through it.

As we got closer to the relocation date, we took time to identify any anxieties they wanted to address. One of those anxieties was the increased volume of business they were expecting at the new store and not knowing how that was going to impact their business and their lives. Another anxiety was the expectation for excellence; they were unsure of how to offer continued support for leadership in the midst of transition. With increased recordkeeping needs, it would be necessary to hire a number of new employees, which meant onboarding. This timeframe also coincided with the local universities' holiday break, which would prove an additional challenge for hiring and training.

Anticipating the likelihood for some unexpected feelings to arise after relocation, we needed to prepare emotionally. I knew there was a strong possibility that after all the lead-up to the relocation there might be a sense of anti-climax when it was completed. I told them to anticipate a feeling of being let down, of being disconnected after the relocation, and sure enough that came to pass. That's not unusual. It's like a team preparing for a big game; there's a lot of intensity and focus, and when it's done they rejoice for a while, and then there's a moment of, 'What do we do next?' The principle applies in business, for an individual, within a marriage or family, and even in ministry. When you extend yourself for a particular cause or project, after it's done and accomplished, even if it's accomplished well, there's a feeling of needing to regain direction. One of the answers is to clarify your vision and develop your goals. Another is to understand that it's normal to step back for a time. We took a two-month break from coaching while they settled into the new location. That enabled them to move past the letdown phase and re-engage; since reengagement they have done phenomenal work.

When we talked about anxieties they were experiencing after relocation, they said they felt the loss of synergy beginning to resurface. Similar to what they were experiencing as a team prior to beginning the coaching process. Another feeling that surfaced was the uncertainty that comes with success and how to deal with that. There were feelings of exhaustion, being overwhelmed, and not knowing the answers to new challenges. One director expressed a sense of loss of control and conflicting directions. None of those were unexpected, but they're serious issues among the team that needed to be addressed. There were two pivotal questions during that period. One was, 'How do you like to be praised and rewarded?' That would help them rebuild some of the synergy they needed. The other question was, 'How do you like to lead and be led?' It was at that time that I introduced to them the "Seven Signs of a Healthy Team Culture" (see page lxvi). This tool was pivotal in refocusing the group toward the future.

Once we reengaged coaching, we revised the weekly director's agenda to further the building of a strong team culture. They developed a standardized agenda format, beginning with a devotional time because of the spiritual heritage of the company. They would list a leadership principle and discuss how it would be applied; they did what they called "**life check-ins,**" relating to one another in a personal way and discussing how they could support one another in their own pilgrimage. They set aside time for "**team talk,**" where they discussed how to develop the larger team in the company, and they had an update on each aspect of the business. They talked about power-moves, the one move in your area of responsibility that would have a positive effect on the company. Once these areas were covered, they moved into action items for the meeting, ending with an action item list. That's a pretty tight meeting; we refer to it as "The Power Hour."

In the midst of all of this, six months into the coaching agreement, we began working on the two-track leadership development plan. Track one follows a new employee through the onboarding process as they learn their particular tasks and which leadership principles apply. Track two is called "Foundations of Flagship," which addresses personal and leadership development. Foundations of Flagship is a ten-session course. (See Session Topics located in Appendix II.) This was developed under the Leadership Development Guide (see Appendix II). This would be the starting point for a personal growth plan, we call it, "Reach Your Potential" (see Appendix V).

By now the directors had started to see real changes in their lives, and at work, that they attributed directly to coaching. At the time, James's goal was to eventually become an owner-operator, in part because he felt that his own operator, Ray, has been so influential in his life. He wanted to have the same influence—employing 100 to 150 people and providing them a safe place to work and a way to provide for their families. He planned to enter into the leadership program and hoped that his coaching work would give him an edge.

There are tools that James learned to use on a daily basis, both in the workplace and in school, whether it's in class, preparing for a test, or scheduling his time over the coming week. For him, coaching was not just about the program or the future, but developing a number of skills that could be applied every day and help him take a more structured approach to the various life challenges. Like many other directors, learning the value of calendaring and your "best yes" was very helpful for James.

"It's hard to balance school, work, and personal life. I've learned that success comes down to time management. I schedule time to relax and even set aside time for naps. Scheduling helps you make the tough decisions with your time." James also struggled with being vulnerable. "A lot of what I need to do requires control. Gary has taught me to empower my team and helped me tell my inside story. If somebody asks me about my day and I just say, 'School work,' then I'm not sharing the whole story. The whole story gives my team an opportunity to really know me and what I'm going through."

"When you say you're on a team, what you usually mean is that there are people you spend a lot of time with every day, but Gary has helped us create a different definition of team, being interconnected with people around you who are making deposits of trust. Every time you 'do what you say, when you say, how you say,' you're making a deposit. When you don't, that person now trusts you less. Why would they depend on you? When your team feels like you're really a team and has that trust, you work *for* someone, not just *with* someone. This is my team, we work for each other every day."

Despite only being twenty-eight years old, much of James's drive and ambition comes from being raised by his grandmother and watching people he cared about struggle in ways he wished they hadn't had to. He came to enjoy working hard and earning what he worked for, and feeling like he had a hand in making something so great. Succeeding in his goals makes him feel like he's fulfilling his purpose and doing something that matters.

Joe summarizes his take on coaching in two words: "Coaching rocks!" and further elaborated by saying, "It's valuable. Coaching in general affected our restaurant in so many positive and unexpected ways that none of us saw when we first signed up. We knew we were starting at the bottom. We knew once we understood that and realized how much we needed to grow, we sometimes doubted whether it was possible. But through trust in our coach, and in one another, we did it, and it was well worth it. I say that "putting a lot of emphasis on *well worth it*. It's worth the journey." On a more granular level, Joe was able to articulate specifically some of the personal discoveries he made through coaching. "Before I was not a planner. I thought I could keep it all in here," he said, pointing to his head. "But frankly, I would forget things and not follow through. It wasn't intentional, I would just forget I had said yes to something and not do it because I had forgotten about it. I would try to keep it in here and just couldn't. I would feel awful about it. Now, if I'm given something to do, I'm like, 'Hold on,' and I put it on the list.' And I don't just put it on the list, but I include when it's going to be done by, because you put a bunch of stuff on the list, and then you look at it all and wonder, 'What do I do first?' Not just writing things down but prioritizing your calendar. Not just planning out when you're going to knock out your to-do list, but planning out your entire week, month, and year. That was a game changer for me. I didn't really think about beforehand."

Joe's leadership style also evolved a great deal. He puts a greater focus on relationships now, and in developing authority with people. Building trust was important, as was leading with authority, and learning how to answer questions like, "What am I doing? Why am I here? Where are we going to go? How are we going to get there?" Answering those important questions, identifying purpose, mission, and vision, actually putting a pinpoint on the board and writing down how he's going to get there. This was a new experience for him. "Actually writing it down and seeing it in front of you is huge."

In addition to the discoveries he made about himself, Joe learned about the inner workings of a team, and the value of speaking into one another's lives. An important part of the process was knowing that he had permission from his team members to ask the tough questions and have the hard conversations, "instead of just firing away." To keep doing things the old way, he realizes now, would have meant a lot of hurt feelings all around. Those tough conversations are necessary, but they're made easier through the coaching process. That has proven to be a valuable way to build others; establishing a coaching culture throughout all levels of the business has been the ultimate objective (see Developing a Coaching Culture in Appendix VI).

Joe saw that once the directors had used the coach approach to build one another to a certain point of improvement, they became able to pay that forward by coaching other employees and building them up in a similar way. Those employees are then able to go on and do the same with others; in this sense, the coach approach creates a ripple effect within an organization by allowing team members on every level to interact in a more positive and productive way. "So now we're seeing the effects on coaching not just on us, but on others as well. So I think that's the biggest win of the coaching process so far." We have developed a form entitled, Development in Coaching, to use as a guide and to strengthen accountability.

Ryan has also reflected on the ways in which coaching has changed him, both personally and professionally. It's allowed him to enhance his communication skills. Before, he was very much a directive leader who had all the answers and people would come to him for those answers. He understands now, that method only gets you so far, because it makes employees very dependent on you. Making that shift, to where he can be their coaching leader rather than the guy with all the answers has been an enormous relief.

Coaching has also helped clarify Ryan's goals for the future. "I had already made the decision not to continue pursuing journalism, but coaching really solidified that. That's when I said, 'Ray, let's do this together. I'm most willing to do whatever you've got in mind for your business,' that's when we signed up for a leadership coach."

Ryan wants to participate in a Chick-fil-A program that moves employees around the country to different locations, depending on their skill set. "Last August I was speaking with a grand-opening supervisor, and he started asking questions about the business that I really didn't know the answers to. Until then I thought that I was ready. I realized that I needed to examine the areas in which I needed to grow. My goal is to be so doggone good that when I interview with corporate for an owner-operator opportunity they'll say, 'Absolutely, yes.'"

When asked to identify the most helpful component of the coaching process, Ryan offered this thoughtful answer. "The personal coaching meetings with Gary. The group meetings were really great as far as helping us with alignment and business and professional growth, but the individual meetings made a significant difference. We were able to jump in and self-reflect, and stop thinking about the outside world and how fast it's moving, that focused me. There are certain tools we've been taught in order to help us be more productive, and the biggest one for me is scheduling. If I can stick to a schedule, sleep well, eat right, that's when I feel like I'm operating at my best potential. And I really value using those tools to teach others. The five people we put through the leadership course are leaps and bounds ahead of other leaders in our restaurant, because we taught them something small, like scheduling. It's up to them if they want to keep it up not. But I think that is the biggest thing that coaching has helped me with, personally and on a professional level, to teach others."

TJ observed that learning more about one another, building relationships, and increasing trust and chemistry were all aspects of the coaching process that improved their ability to work together as a team and tackle challenges like the relocation. "Coaching helped us set our goals and expectations with clarity and purpose. We all communicated set goals of when and how we would execute, to be prepared for the relocation. Supporting one another individually and as a team, all this combined helped us to be prepared and hit the ground running at the new store."

As for keeping up these positive changes in the future, Ray said that the focus on character will remain a cornerstone of the store's culture. "We will obviously continue to focus on character. That's in the thread of everything we talk about, all the time now. Because of coaching, there are a couple things that we practice on a daily basis in the business. We use *carefrontations* versus *confrontations*. So when we have conversations with our staff and talk about opportunities for bettering themselves in their work area, we do it with love, care, and encouragement, versus criticism or negativity. We try to share with them in positive ways to encourage them and help them grow. The other thing that we do, and we're getting much better at, is developing our coaching culture. That is, asking questions to help people to start thinking on their own versus always telling them the answer. 'Be a clock builder versus a time teller.' There's lots of different ways to do it, but the coaching culture is what we've grabbed onto with Gary and what we're actively practicing. We already understood our communication challenges. It's difficult to get information from here to there effectively, but we're finding it to be easier through this process."

"I think for our particular situation it's challenging because of the various transitions we have experienced, going from that store to this store (relocation), trying to prepare for a potential second store, while we're also figuring out how to handle significant growth. It's a lot to be happening all at one time. With my team it's important to make sure we take temperatures of the team to see what their tolerance level is. I'm learning what kind of stress I put them under and how much is too much. I've learned to regulate."

As the directors and the rest of the employees settled into the new restaurant, a plan began to take shape for the possible second store. Down the road, the old building remains vacant; if—or when—Ray receives approval from corporate to take on a second Chick-fil-A franchise, the former location would be leased again, and reopened as a drive-through only restaurant, a complement to the full service location currently operating on Archer Road. As they continue to hit their goals and reach their milestones, this is coming closer and closer to becoming a reality. All the lessons learned about managing transitions—the anticipation and anxiety, the loss of synergy and its subsequent recapture—will be put to use again to handle the challenges of reaching this next level of success.

"Trusting you is my decision, proving me right is your choice."
— *Unknown*

Bumps in the Road Lead to Refocusing

"Trust is a fragile thing."

— *Unknown*

Despite all the progress we had made through coaching, it was by no means a seamless transition to a coaching culture that placed so much value on trust and character. After the transition to the new location was complete, the team began to set their sights on the goal of opening a second location. We continued individual and group coaching sessions, and it seemed for a time as though all major transitions were over, and everyone could take a breath.

We were wrong.

Instead, the team of directors were both shocked and saddened when their trust was broken by one of their own. James had violated company policy and was subject to immediate termination. As everyone struggled to cope with this deep personal betrayal, they were also saddled with a heightened workload as they suddenly found themselves a member short. Rather than being able to enjoy their growing success, they had to reckon with all the complicated feelings that came from his abrupt departure. This betrayal of trust threatened all their hard-earned progress, not to mention the extra work each took on to cover the now vacant position. Through coaching they processed this devastating development, and worked to refocus and find their way forward toward achieving their goals.

As the talent development director, it fell to Misty to give Ray the terrible news that James had violated policy and would need to be let go. It filled her with both a deep sadness and anger. Ray, who had invested so much of himself in James, personally and professionally, was heartbroken to learn about the situation.

"Of all the things that have happened in the past year, this is the one that has upset me the most," Misty said. "Having to call Ray and tell him about James was incredibly hard for me, because Ray's commitment and care for James was so deep. I hated having to be the one to call Ray and tell him that he had been betrayed. One of the hardest things I ever had to do was terminate a fellow director. In disbelief I thought, 'What?' This is somebody that sat around the leadership table with me."

It was one of the hardest things Ray had to do as well, so together Misty and Ray met with James. They had to draw the line by saying, "No matter who you are, if we can't trust you to follow the policies and procedures, you can't work here." James was someone who had a long tenure. There were lots of heartstrings, and growth had happened, just not enough. Ray and Misty understood that misalignment would not get the team to where they needed to go.

Ryan agreed that this violation was one of the biggest challenges that the team had faced together. In the past, when there had been a break in trust, the team shied away from it or avoided tackling it in some way, even if they knew or suspected that something problematic was happening. Once James was no longer sitting around the table with the other directors, "it made us more aware as a team of what we won't accept. We have to push each other to be better."

In addition to handling the emotional fallout of losing James, other directors and employees had to scramble to pick up the extra workload left behind after losing such a senior team member on short notice. Rather than rush through the process of bringing in another director right away, the others pitched in, but this created its own hardships and a few hurt feelings. Joe described what made him angriest after James's abrupt departure.

"When I found out what a giant hole I had been left to dig out of this spring, and how much work was in front of me, that was hard to absorb. It was the combination of the trust violation and the workload consequences. There were a lot of things to do, a lot that fell on my plate. Taking on additional responsibilities and having to do all the heavy lifting because it hadn't been done."

This illustrates a crucial point, that the cultural idea, "what I do is my business, and my life is none of your business," is false. Everything we do, every choice we make, impacts somebody else. It's just a matter of how deeply and how far-ranging that impact occurs. In the case of James, his choices impacted the entire team, in a very negative way. His departure threatened to disrupt the culture of trust and character that had been developed over time, and coaching work shifted, once again, to focusing on these core elements.

Joe made a series of observations about building trust through the coaching process. "You have to start with identifying the major issues at hand, and for us a big thing was trust. It was keeping us from developing better interpersonal relationships with one another and at the restaurant. It was keeping us from working to our full potential, and it was hampering our productivity. Getting over that hump was a huge turning point, and once we did that, we were actually able to start coaching. That was step number one, and I think that was the biggest win, the fact that the team was finally able to trust one another, or so we thought.

They thought James was going to live up to their culture of character and all of the values the directors had established together. It was a policy they'd had in place for almost a year at that point, and it was a policy James himself supported and had helped enforce in the past.

Joe recalled the meeting that took place after James's termination and his efforts, as well as those of his colleagues, to accept the shocking news. "We had a meeting right after it happened. We were very upset. I was shocked because I had worked with James for a long time. We started at CFA Archer Road within a week of each other. It just hurt. It really did. But in the end we came out better from it. The policy implementation was consistent with our values. It had a kind of self-cleaning effect to it, and there were people that self-selected out and that's been for the best. There were also people that took their chances breeching the policy and ended up having to leave. It forced some people to make lifestyle changes to be in alignment with the policy. Those that are still with us today are in leadership positions higher than they ever would have attained had we stuck with our old ways."

As the executive director, Ryan was also affected by the loss of personnel, despite his support of strict policies that reinforce the culture of character. "We're more aware as a team of what we can't accept, and how we have to push one another forward."

Months after James's departure, the directors hired someone who they had hoped would soon fill the Kitchen Manager position. There was some initial excitement around finally filling that role. However, once again they experienced a sense of disappointment when this individual changed his mind about accepting the position at the last minute—over text message, no less. This time the team was better prepared though, and worked through it together.

As surprising as it was to have someone decline the position over text message, using the coaching strategies that helped the directors navigate James's departure meant that this time it was not a major disruption. We had spent additional time implementing those principles and steps of building trust that we used in our initial work together, processing those and asking, 'How does this apply now that trust has been broken?' That was a helpful way to rebuild trust.

?
Coaching
Questions

Over time they were able to find the right person for the role, and the position was filled by a young man named Selvin. He had been working in the kitchen for about seven or eight years. He has a wonderful story. During our first session I just listened as he shared his journey. Chick-fil-A has played a major role in giving his life direction, focus, and learning opportunities. When Ray promoted him to this pivotal position, Selvin was excited and committed to making it work. After years of hard work, he is now sitting around the directors' table.

Ryan made a very insightful observation about working with people who lack character or intentionally disappoint others.

"When we have someone who we absolutely can't trust, they eventually will find a way out. The dishonesty will eventually come out, because the rest of us are all working toward the same goals, with the same mindset, the same alignment. Coaching first put us on the same page; otherwise we could have kept brushing it under the rug and letting it be. Instead, we decided that wasn't how we're going to operate anymore. For example, if I were to fail at something now, my director team would let me know rather than just let it slide, which we used to do."

There are other matters that no effective organization can "just let slide." These come from toxic people. We can all be toxic at times, but a toxic person has unhealthy patterns and they don't want or aren't willing, to get better. As a result they can be consistently negative and critical, making few, if any significant contributions. They quietly, passively, or sometimes even aggressively, oppose. Toxicity may be expressed by constantly underperforming, blaming others or specific circumstances for their lack of performance. Another example of a toxic person is one with a hidden or conflicting agenda conflicting with the stated vision. This person drains time and energy from the team. The best response to these issues is a clear statement, "It won't be tolerated." That's the only alternative if the person can't be trusted for positive change.

This experience is a dramatic demonstration of the essential nature of trust. It has been said that "everything rises or falls on leadership." It is my persuasion that "everything rises or falls on trust - even leadership." This is underscored by the following article.

Questions for Personal and Professional Growth
- Why is the violation of trust so painful and disruptive?
- How does a "culture of character" provide the foundation for trust?
- What is a healthy response to the violation of trust?

★ ★ ★

According to the following multi-year Harvard University study on "trust" in which they measured both the working conditions and brain chemicals for "trust levels," researchers discovered some revealing facts that can be helpful wanting to increase the level of trust within personal and professional relationships (Levin 2017).

PWC's 2016 Global CEO Survey revealed that 50 percent of CEOs worldwide consider lack of trust to be a major threat to their organizational growth.

Paul J. Zak, Harvard researcher, Founding Director of the Center for Neuroeconomics Studies and Professor of Economics, Psychology and Management at Claremont Graduate University, and author of *The Trust Factor: The Science of Creating High Performing Companies*, has invested decades researching the neurological connection between trust, leadership, and organizational performance.

Here is a summary of the article and where it can be found:

Over his two decades of research, Zak discovered that "compared with people at low-trust companies, people at high-trust companies report 74 percent less stress, 106 percent more energy at work, 50 percent higher productivity, 13 percent fewer sick days, 76 percent more engagement, 29 percent more satisfaction with their lives, and 40 percent lessburnout."

Here are Zak's eight strategies for creating cultures of trust:

- Recognize excellence—Public recognition builds trust.
- Induce "challenge stress"—Challenges must follow the SMART model: Specific, Measurable, Attainable, Realistic, and Time-Sensitive with a deadline.
- Empower employees to choose their work patterns and habits—Autonomy over work conditions communicates to employees that their leadership trusts them. A Citigroup and LinkedIn survey found that nearly half of employees would forfeit a 20 percent raise for greater control over their work environment.
- Give employees a voice in their own job design—This freedom allows them to select projects that most closely align with their strongest skill sets and professional passions.
- Communicate often—Thorough and frequent communication is one of the easiest ways to gain employee loyalty and trust. Gallup polled 2.5 million manager-led

teams in 195 countries and found that daily communication with direct reports measurably improved workforce engagement.

- Intentionally build relationships—Gallup has found that having a best friend at work significantly increases workplace engagement. The study revealed that those that felt they had friends at work were 43 percent more likely to report having received recognition for their work, which we know stimulates more oxytocin and drives more happiness. A LinkedIn study revealed that almost 50 percent of professionals believe that having work-friends is critical to their overall happiness.

- Facilitate whole-person growth—Employers who recognize that employees are multi-dimensional and are interested in comprehensive personal and professional development beyond technical development will have a competitive advantage over those that don't. The Bersin by Deloitte *Future of Corporate Learning Report* revealed that millennials are "desperate for learning" and rank training and development as the #1 desired job benefit, above flexible schedules and money.

- Show vulnerability—The organizations with the highest trust recognize that asking for help is a two-way street. The most emotionally connected leaders let their employees know that they need their help to build the best organizations possible.

The Impact of Trust on the Bottom Line

The quantitative results of a trust-based culture were remarkable. Zak concluded that those working in high-trust cultures:

- Enjoyed their jobs 60 percent more
- Were 70 percent more aligned with their companies' purpose
- Felt 66 percent closer to their colleagues
- Had 11 percent more empathy for their workmates
- Experienced 40 percent less burnout from their work
- Earn an additional $6,450 a year, or 17 percent more than those working at low-trust organizations

Science has spoken. Trust is no longer optional for organizations that want to attract and retain the best people and want to achieve the best results (Levin 2017).

★ ★ ★

"Successful people do what unsuccessful people are not willing to do. Don't wish it were easier; wish it were better."

— *Jim Rohn*

Questions for Personal and Professional Impact
- How does getting at your "inside story" relate to goal setting?
- What does "carefronting" mean and how does this apply in your relationships?
- What is the "confessional" approach to communication and why is it so powerful?

PART THREE

AMPLIFY

"The key is measurement, simple as that."
—*Roberth D. Hare*
Professor, University of British Columbia

5

MEASURE

"The quality of a leader is reflected in the standards they set for themselves."
— Ray Kroc

T he third pricinple in this coaching model is to *amplify.* 💡
Amplify means to apply in order to grow (expand, enlarge, increase). This chapter will reveal, through the individual lens of each team member, how the coach approach continues to work in and through their lives.

After I had been working with the directors for about a year, they had overcome a number of challenges and achieved real growth. All their hard work has led to real change and tangible success. They've created a coaching culture within the organization that has allowed them to encourage and duplicate leadership. By applying their focus and energy to enable this growth, they've used their attitude and knowledge to create a set of positive outcomes that can be measured by the store's increased sales and improved customer experience. Individually, they have each reflected on the positive outcomes they've seen as they continue to work toward their ultimate goal of flagship.

"I don't know if they were discoveries or amplifiers of things I already knew," Misty said. "Trust issues, time management. Finding my best yes. If I say yes to something, I'm saying no to something else. If I say yes to an interview at seven pm, I'm saying no to dinner with my family. That was a big discovery for me; I'd never seen it from that perspective."

Misty has also learned how to trust herself and believe she does have the skills that other people tell her she has, like leadership skills and the ability to talk in front of other people—even though she's not too fond of the latter. Coaching has given her a way to competently talk to others and make those conversations productive ones. Now, when she sits down to have a conversation with someone, using the coach approach they can arrive at a best answer, create a list of action items, and she can offer them whatever support they need. She can let them know they're not alone in getting there, and she can give them the right tools. Everyone walks away with a clear idea of what the next steps are.

"The coach approach is what I use to help people find the best answer to a problem or a question; it doesn't always have to be something based around a negative experience. It could just be about growth. It is the best answer to finding the best answer."

One of the most helpful parts of the process for Misty is working with action items; having tangible next steps instead of vague or abstract ideas about how to move forward. She described how the directors incorporated these into their meetings so that everyone leaves knowing exactly which tasks they are responsible for prior to the group coming together again. "At the end, after we get to the best answer, we come up with ways to actually implement that best answer. Getting to the best answer was definitely the most difficult part, but I need to know how to apply that. I need to know what to do next."

Another challenge Misty has tackled is creating boundaries and sticking to them. She programs her phone so she can't receive calls or texts after 11:15 p.m., fifteen minutes after the store closes, or before 6:30 a.m., half an hour after the store opens. During that period of time, there shouldn't be any dire emergencies requiring her attention. She created another boundary on Sundays, when she'll read messages but not respond to them. She communicates these boundaries clearly to others, so their expectations are aligned with her schedule.

Laura addressed how she felt the coaching culture changed their work environment as a whole. From her perspective, the overall change has been a positive one, albeit still a work in progress. CFA Archer Road now employs over 150 people, with new ones coming through the door every day. Those employees are being empowered by the coaching process, which helps them find their own best answers, and by being on the receiving end of a constant filter of information that makes them happier and more confident.

She also described certain parts of the process, the actual nuts and bolts of coaching, that she found particularly productive. "Gary had expectations coming into our sessions. 'I want you to know what you want to focus on today, what you want to coach around today.' Getting to that point, really figuring out, 'What is it that I need?' Getting to something that I'm unable to get to by myself. That's been very impactful after getting through the basics of figuring out my vision, my purpose, all of those things. Sometimes Gary would give us the tools and sometimes he'd make us think through, 'Okay, well, what tools do you need?' He's always asking the right questions. And then he turned the tables and made us coach. 'Okay, now you're going to be part of a triad, where you're going to be the coach, this person is going to be the coachee, and that person is going to be the one who observes.'

Coaching Questions "We're learning about ourselves. We're really getting to the bottom of, 'Who are you in this process? What are your beliefs and how are you going to make this your path in life? What tools do you need? How does this get better for you?'

Laura also reflected on how coaching has affected her life outside of work. She's learned that while her work and her personal life is different, she is always the same person. She's here to serve others, but at the same time she never wants to stop growing and pursuing new things. Perhaps part of that comes from being a mom. "One day my daughter asked me, 'What are your dreams, Mom?' and I told her I had stopped dreaming a long time ago. I really thought about it afterward, why did I say that to her? She's seventeen, she's dreaming, she's doing all this stuff, why did I ever say that to her? I told her, 'Well, my dreams used to be this, this, and this, but I found my prince and I have two beautiful princesses, I have a lot of those things. It's not like I'm yearning to go do something else because

I want to be here with you.' I guess I scared the mud out of her. I let myself reflect on that a little bit, and it's led to this decision to continue to pursue things and not say, 'Okay, I'm good right here.' You have a lot more life ahead of you to do different things. So she challenged me in that way, to discover that, but I probably wouldn't have been open to it had Gary not used the hammer to crack open my stubbornness."

The focus on coaching culture—both at home and at work— had changed Laura's ideas about what leadership is. They don't need them to just stand in the front and say, "Do this, do that, do this." They need strong coach managers that they can trust to help them. "They need our support to grow. We've started that process with the leadership development plan and bringing them in on some of the things that we've had the opportunity to learn under Gary. They don't all get that opportunity firsthand, but it's our responsibility to trickle that down. They need the tools from us to succeed. Sometimes we think, 'Oh, we don't have what we need.' But we do have what we need. Sometimes we're just not using it. So we need to make sure that we are giving them the tools and that they look to us for their next step, and we need to be prepared for what that is. When they're ready and they're waiting on you, it's too late."

Restructuring the marketing department was another tangible takeaway that came out of the coaching process. They recently developed a new marketing program called the B.R.I.D.G.E. Team (see B.R.I.D.G.E. in Appendix IV). It brings together employees from different working areas of the restaurant. Their goals are different than just the marketing team's; they're also encouraging one another and bringing some cohesiveness across the board. That idea came from Misty and Laura. "We said, 'Hey, let's create something different that they can coach each other through and make an impact. That's one of the most important results the coaching culture has had on marketing, because it's different. I'm not teaching everybody every day, I'm giving them the tools, and the resources, and then saying, 'These are the things we want you to do.'"

Staying organized and keeping up with all her tasks remains a challenge. As Laura said, "I've got twelve things on my list. If I'm not prioritizing my time well, then Gary and I work together to help me find organization in my life, because a lot of times I was feeling overwhelmed. Working with a coach really helps to focus you and get you on track with your own personal goals, which a lot of times get skewed just in general. I'm a wife, I'm a mom, I'm busy with my church. My brother always asks me, 'Have you said no yet?' The coaching experience personally has brought things more into focus about goals. A goal is something you're taking steps toward. Where do you want to go? Have you thought about how you're going to get there? Those organizational questions help to focus me. With corporate leadership, I think it just brought us together in a way nothing else had before."

TJ also found that strengthening his organizational skills had a powerful impact that radiated throughout both his personal and professional life. "That was where I had the most room for growth; calendaring and using it as a tool in my life. Before working with

Gary that tool was non-existent for me. I was not a planner. I would put stuff in my calendar but I wasn't using it as a tool. I would look at it, but if you look at this bottle of water and don't drink it, it's not going to do you any good, you're just going to be thirsty and dehydrated and unable to perform to your potential.

"I was not prioritizing my time very well. I learned when I put together my calendar to rank things as most important, least important, to write things out. I sat down and put some thought into it, and started planning ahead. Gary challenged me to do a week, and by the time I got done, before I knew it I was a month ahead. The very first time I'd ever done it. That was huge for me. And then I saw the smile on Gary's face and that made it even more worthwhile."

Ray discovered that the elements of coaching that he enjoyed the least, were also the ones he found most effective. "Accountability," he said. "It's the one I liked the least, but it's the one that works the best. Isn't that so often the way? All the other ones sound fancy and are nice, but accountability is what makes it happen at the end of the day. Without it, it's easy to slack off and not finish the stuff you need to complete. So amongst all the other tools that coaching provides, for me accountability is the most important."

His growth as a leader has allowed him the pleasure of witnessing that growth in others. One of the greatest joys for Ray is when a former team member comes back and brings their kids in to share what's going on in their world. That success fills him up, to know that maybe the business, or Ray personally, had something to do with where they are today. "Sometimes they come back and say, 'This was the most rewarding job I've had,' or something of that nature. Or, 'When I was here, I learned this that helped me,' that fuels me to want to continue to do what I do. Continue to build and develop people." This is true for Ray at home as well. "I can't wait to see my daughter graduate college. She's going to be a sophomore this year. I've got another daughter who's going to start second grade. Looking to the future, I want to grow more leaders."

It's always interesting to compare Ray and Ryan's observations; the former is the established operator and the latter is the aspiring leader. Observing how Ray handles his businesses and team members has given Ryan a strong reference point for where he wants to be someday. He expressed his gratitude for Ray's willingness to make the investment in his team. "Ray gave us something as a business owner to help us grow further than what he could have done alone. He's great with keeping us accountable, teaching me about the business, helping me grow as a leader in Chick-fil-A, and passing on everything he's learned. I've worked for different CFA owner-operators before, but I've never seen them invest in their team the way Ray does." Ray is unique. He's at the store all the time. He wants to see us grow and he wants to facilitate that growth."

We determined the **Five Critical Success Factors**:

- Vision
- People
- Quality & Customer Experience
- Sales & Brand Growth
- Financial Return

As the numbers indicate, managing the Five Critical Success Factors well yields exceptional financial returns, finishing 2018 at seven million, setting a 2019 goal for nine million, and ultimately achieving 9.8 million.

Working with Misty on leadership development has already put Ryan in a position to start passing on what he's learned. "Misty and I have very different outlooks on life or things that we would be looking for first when identifying other potential leaders. But with the tools that we've learned through coaching, we're able to play off each other when we're teaching others how to be a coach, how to use the coach approach, how to find solutions in the workplace and outside of the workplace, just through our own experiences with coaching. For example, we'll have a coaching triad, where somebody will coach, someone will be the coachee, and then we'll have an observer. We were able to do that with a group of five people who were already put through the leadership course, and they are now actively coaching one another in the restaurant, actively coaching others to the point where they're exceeding their other leaders or supervisors in coaching and in growth. Just because we've had the opportunity to use what we've learned and coach others."

Despite all this enormous growth, Ryan does still experience frustration when he occasionally finds himself reverting back to old habits. He relies heavily on the communication skills he's learned, not just with his team but also with the people around him in his life. "If I ever revert back to the old Ryan or the old way of doing things, where I just take on everything by myself, eventually one of the plates will fall, and that's when I would break down emotionally.

So I need to continue communication with others, continue communication with Jesus. If I ever revert back to not doing that, that's when I break."

Even his responses to these occasional moments, however, have been altered. "In the past, showing emotion at all would be something I would stay away from. I was afraid it would make me seem weak to others, or a sign that, 'Wow, this person can't do their job, get back on the line.' Now I accept it and run toward it. Because that's the only way I'm going to grow. We're all going to fail at times, but we can fail forward rather than retreating back into what we knew or did before. It's okay to be emotional. Obviously not when we're serving a guest, but there are a lot of times we deal with emotion inside the restaurant. Often the team members take the brunt of it when a guest is angry or disappointed, and they bring it to me. I walk up to the guest and they say, 'Hi, of course, thanks so much.' So I rarely get to experience guest satisfaction except through the team. So knowing that I've been there before and helping them through their emotions at the time is something I would not have done previously."

For somebody like Joe, who is always eager to interact with others and share what he knows, the coach approach has given him a more structured way to model leadership and pass on lessons that he knows will encourage growth. "I'm a talker. There are a few of us who really like to talk. Anytime we would try to have those conversations to build people up, it would end with rambling or vague closed-ended questions. Now we are asking clear, open-ended questions. That's the foundation of coaching itself, is teaching through asking questions.

Like the other directors, Joe has seen positive outcomes in his personal life as well. "Planning out my life, writing things down, planning out when I'm going to do things, that was a huge help. That was an identifiable gap for me. Learning how to articulate things properly, that was something we focused on for a couple of weeks, articulating our stories, sharing my inside story. During interviews I'll get asked, 'Tell me your story, tell me about yourself,' and I learned through Gary how to effectively tell my story. You have to know, even if it's not that interesting, how to make it interesting and emotionally charged at some level. I learned how to do that, and I don't think I could have done that without help."

Using his new powers of articulation, Joe expressed why he found coaching to be a more effective approach to personal growth. "It makes you create your own plans to grow, and it makes you think of those ways to grow on your own. You're not just told, this is what you need to do to grow yourself personally; you're asked questions and challenged to summarize it at the end. At the very end of the coaching session, I know what I need to do to improve my personal life or the professional goal that I'm working towards. I never thought of that going in. I just thought this guy was going to help improve my leadership style. Instead I'm learning how to answer those questions on my own."

Joe also recognizeds the value in passing on the investment. "When you're coaching, it shows that you're committed to that individual's growth instead of just giving them the answer in a nice, long ramble. You're asking them the questions that show them you're really trying to help them, instead of just a quick, 'All right, here you go.' You're taking the time to help them find the answer, so it shows commitment from one person to the other and that improves the relationship."

TJ elaborated on this sentiment. "The employees wanted more development opportunities, because we were investing in showing interest in them, so as people started seeing that it created a ripple effect. I didn't realize how much they relied on us. We have great people who are reaching their potential through the plans Ryan and Misty have worked on so diligently. I've learned that there's room for growth for everybody. There's always room for continuous growth with leaders at all levels."

This has changed the entire atmosphere of the business. The directors have been invested in, and now they are investing in others. They get to build people up, because coaching lets people know they're being invested in. By building strength that is then passed onto others using the same coaching methods, they've built trust and strength in their relationships, and improved their performance by aligning their goals as a team.

"It's also helped me as a person," says TJ. It helped me with planning, structure, and learning about myself. One of the first things we were asked was, 'What do you want to coach around?' It was left to us what we thought we needed. It's also impacted my spiritual life. In addition to relying on my faith, it's helped me build trust and rely on my spiritual relationships instead of trying to tackle it by myself. I worry less. I'm not as stressed compared to before. When I start to get emotional I can channel it into something productive compared to the alternative, which is worry and stress and being negatively affected by the outcome. I went from always worrying to staying positive through constant prayer. I've been seeking out ways to serve at my church. I'm currently almost a year into becoming a men's ministry leader."

TJ's long tenure at Chick-fil-A has given him a unique perspective. "I've been at Chick-fil-A on Archer Road since 2001, so I've seen different managers that have grown leaders, and now I'm on the other end of the spectrum, growing leaders that are potentially going to go on to operate their own store one day."

One thing that you can do to help measure your effectiveness, individually or as a team, is to use the **PSWOT Analysis** (Personal Strenghs, Weaknesses, Opportunities, and Threats). The PSWOT Analysis is credited to Albert Humphrey, a business and management consultant.

Your PSWOT Analysis should be based on both internal and external feedback. This will provide you with a lot of helpful information. Determine which strengths apply to specific opportunities. Use your strengths to neutralize threats. It is most helpful to focus on your strengths. Your weaknesses can show you where not to invest your major time and energy.

Many tools are available for measurement, but the one principle is this - there must be accurate measurement for consistent progress toward a preferred future.

★ ★ ★

"One measure is worth a thousand expert opinions."

—*Donald Sutherland*

Questions for Personal and Professional Impact
- What were some of the successful outcomes of coaching the individual team members?
- What are some of the successful outcomes for the collective team?
- What were some of the successful outcomes for the business?

"What lies behind us, and what lies before us, are but tiny matters compared to what lies within us."

— *Ralph Waldo Emerson*

6

COACHING =
ENDLESS SELF-DISCOVERY

"Growth is not about discovering yourself, it's about discovering who God created you to become."

— Unknown

A s I coached the directors, I learned that even personally, the self-discoveries are endless. Coaching acts as a mirror that you hold up to yourself; encouraging someone to ask themselves a series of questions to find their best answer also means that you will inevitably turn those same questions inward for reflection yourself. If you're going to coach with integrity and consistency, you have to ask yourself where you are as well. I discovered through this experience the power and enjoyment of coaching from a business point of view, and I've also enjoyed the ability to connect in personal and professional ways. I've seen the power of clear vision and strategy, and knowing I need to apply the same priciples consistently in my own life. I've learned how much I enjoy helping people reach their dreams. To really be effective you have to own the process and enter it deeply.

I've seen growth in personal and team confidence, growth in them trusting themselves and their abilities, trusting the team. I've seen them grow in excitement and anticipation. They had two of the three necessary visits from corporate, and both of them have gone extremely well. During the last visit two people came and affirmed Ray by saying, "you and your team have crushed it." It's not certain that they'll get the second store but things are looking very positive in that direction. They'll have a third visit, and if they do get the second store they have determined that the old location will be restored and become a drive-thru only location. So they'll have a drive-thru location less than a mile down the road from their full-service restaurant where they are now. That will be their next major opportunity of growth.

Over the next five years I expect that there will be a continuation of a strong coaching culture. People will grow personally and professionally. Because of the store's location in a college town, a lot of employees will eventually move on to other jobs; some may be within Chick-fil-A and some may not, but if you think about it, they will be influencing communities across the nation.

I've seen each person experience an enormous amount of growth during our work together. Ray has come to be at peace with himself as never before, for two primary reasons. The first is that he made a personal commitment to Christ and that has had a powerful effect on his spiritual life. The second is that he has become much more confident in himself as an owner and as a leader through this process.

Misty is very intuitive and perceptive. Misty has found a different level of courage and confidence, confidence in her intuition and courage to lead from that intuition.

Laura has a more jovial personality, more impromptu. These last few months she has encountered some personal challenges, and she's gained confidence to deal with those challenges. With the relocation and the potential for two stores she's had a pretty significant role change, and she's engaging this opportunity with clarity and confidence, which she could not have in the past. The word for Laura is *organized*. I've seen a significant change in her organizational skills and how that has been applied to her life and work.

Ryan has become the executive director, and I've seen something holistic happen with Ryan. He's really seen the value of the leadership development plan; so for Ryan I'd say we've seen executive changes in him. He's doing incredible work.

Joe has seen growth in his sense of security and confidence in himself to follow through. For Joe the defining word is *consistency*. He's engaged in the corporate leadership development program to become an owner. He may not be with us for that much longer, but wherever he goes he'll take confidence and consistency with him.

TJ is such a nice guy. He's responsible for facilities management and really stepped up to the plate during the relocation. TJ has a broader understanding of business and relational principles.

Selvin sees the great potential in his position and the opportunity afforded to him with the coaching process. Selvin is grateful and excited.

Joe made some observations about how he's internalized these changes and growth. "Learning the difference between power and authority—that power is using your position over others to have them do as you wish, versus authority, which is developing a relationship with those people and their working with you and listening to you based on that relationship. That was really powerful, and it helped increase my relationship-building skills right off the bat. It helped me be more intentional; it made me want to learn more about the people I'm leading. You can't just have a relationship with them, you need to learn more about them so you can empathize and help them grow in any way that you can. It's been phenomenal to find out what people are going through, talk to them, and empathize with them. It's made me ask more questions in my personal life; I want to find out more in each relationship, with my parents, with my girlfriend. How can I strengthen these relationships by finding out more about what's going on with the other person?

"It's helped me wake up to know what my purpose is. Setting a purpose—where do you want to be?—and defining a path—how are you going to get there? Gary worked with Ray to set that up, and we created our own vision for the store, defining why we're doing what we're doing and where we want to be and how we're going to get there. One word: flagship. Being the flagship store for Chick-fil-A, that's Ray's vision. Every restaurant chain has their flagship store and for Chick-fil-A, one of these days, it's going to be the CFA Archer Road store. Coaching has helped define where we're at and showed us where we need to be and what values we need to get there."

TJ shared how these personalized coaching techniques have impacted him. "Any time Gary and I have coached around something he's willingly showed me how he applies it in his own life. TJ took this teaching technique and applied it to the people in his life who look to him for guidance. "I had the challenge of not only doing that for myself, but urging our children who were struggling in high school. So I used that exact model. I took out my calendars and showed them, 'This is what my calendar looks like.' When Gary and I started coaching, my son Trey was having test anxiety and I was trying to help him through that. His frustration was causing me frustration, and that really wasn't helping the situation. So I started showing him how I would plan and set out my week, and I urged him to do the same so he could improve his outcome. He went from struggling with Cs and Ds during his junior year, and his grades started progressing to Bs and Cs, and then he started working on As and Bs, because he knew for his college applications he needed to get his GPA up as high as he could. From his sophomore to his senior year, he brought his GPA up from 1.5 to 3.0. He doubled it, and his victories and success helped me figure out not only did I do something, but I coached him on how to do it. It's made our relationship even stronger."

Ray has been able to truly clarify his life's purpose through coaching. "When Gary said, 'Hey, what is your life's purpose?' I wasn't necessarily able to articulate that, as a lot of people are. If you'd asked me what was my reason for getting up in the morning, I didn't really know. I was just going through the motions the best I could for each day, and when that day was over I would start the next day. So identifying my purpose—saying it out loud and writing it down—really helped focus my energies and efforts on what I wanted to do and how I was going to do it. He let us sit on it for a little while until we could figure out exactly what we wanted to do. I was finally able to articulate my passion and understand that my purpose is to build others to be the best versions of themselves, professionally and personally. That's what I strive to do, and through coaching I'm able to learn how to do that better, and have more time and energy to spend on that. Now when I wake up in the morning, I'm thinking, 'Who do we grow today? What are we doing today?' versus 'I'm just going to get in there, see what happens, and just deal with the day as it comes.'"

In addition to being more intentional, coaching has deepened Ray's emotional intelligence by helping him identify his strengths, which he characterizes as harmony, adaptability, significance, developer, and empathy. "I'm pretty in tune with how I feel about myself. I already knew I wasn't the smartest guy in the room, depending on the room, but I do feel like I have a gift for understanding how people feel or what's going on. I don't always have it to the level of depth that I need to, but I feel like I understand when somebody is feeling stressed or somebody feels like they're in need of something. Now I feel like I'm more equipped in how to handle that and help them through it. Now I have the opportunity to do something about it, versus not knowing what to say or what to do."

In terms of moving forward, Ray has set certain goals for the immediate future, including this book and the second store. "We're working very hard to get ready for that, so we're in the midst of this new challenge right now. My other professional goals are to keep finding and growing more leaders to help us as our business continues to grow. We're going to hopefully add the second store, and we're going to basically double the overhead as far as employees, and so we're trying hard to become very systematic in what we do. We're trying to create repeatable types of opportunities in the business to make it easier for our folks, so we can continue looking for ways to simplify business so we can increase morale and gain some clarity." While there are some opportunities for growth, the size of Gainesville does limit, to some extent, the number of stores that can exist here. "They're looking at other markets, emerging markets. They consider this an existing market. They're trying to get into other places that have no or very little existing brand awareness."

Ray is grateful for the conversation he had with the operator who originally suggested hiring a coach for his team. "I don't know that I would have ever entertained the idea of doing it for myself, much less for my team, had he not been there. I'm so grateful to him for helping me through that discussion, putting me in a place where I was looking into that and wanting to do that. I'm so appreciative of the relationship that Gary and I have, because through that relationship we can be very transparent with each other. Just like when you go to see a doctor, if you don't tell the doctor exactly what's going on, you're not going to get the right diagnosis. So if I don't feel comfortable enough with our relationship to tell him exactly what's going on with me personally and professionally, he's not going to be able to coach me through that process. So I'm extremely thankful for that."

"I feel like we're still in our early stages of coaching, honestly, because everything we've had to do has been systematic, and while we've had a lot of great coaching, we still have a lot more to go, so I'm looking forward to this relationship continuing for quite a while. It's exciting. We're bringing a new director on board and he'll immediately be coaching with Gary. And these guys, I think they enjoy this as a benefit of the business. I think they have started to see the fruits of it."

For Ray, another one of the fruits of coaching that he's been able to enjoy is watching the relationships his team has developed with one another. "I don't know if I could pinpoint the day, but when I saw my director team, these directors, interacting with one another about things that had nothing to do with work, just having fun conversations, laughing, joking, enjoying the relationships they had built, that was incredible. They had gone out as a group and the next time they went they invited me to join them, and that was another great moment. From that standpoint I felt like, okay, things are going in the right direction. Things are good. Together, we can do anything. There's passion. It's not all organizational procedures. It's not all policies and procedures."

Laura has also found clarity of purpose through this process. Before coaching, she did not have an identifiable life's purpose. "It's actually made me analyze it and create one. Before it was just, well, this is kind of who I think I am, but until I was asked, 'What is your life's purpose?' I couldn't have told you. If you'd asked me, I would have been dumbfounded. So basically Gary asked the right questions and I figured out who I knew I was. So now, if I'm asked, I would say, I'm a servant. Not in a bad way, not like, 'Mom, go get me this.' I'm going to serve others so that it builds them up. Coaching has helped clarify my vision and strategy. 'Okay, this is what you say you want. Are you going to go for it? Are you going to do the things that lead you in that direction? It clarified things for me."

Ryan reflected on how the experience defied all his expectations. "When Ray said, 'We're going to get a coach,' I responded, 'Sounds great!' Through having a coach, my growth has been entirely upward. I said before I thought I was ready to be a Chick-fil-A operator, now I think that I have a long way to go before I'm where I want to be. Obviously no one's ever going to be perfect. But I can keep growing, and help others grow. We've had experiences that have been difficult, and Gary is able to see from an outside perspective to help us grow. He frames our lives in a way that's different, that pushes us to be better. That's who Gary is. Someone who's invested in not only his own life and journey, but others' lives and journeys. He forces you out of your comfort zone, makes you feel uncomfortable. He told us up front, 'This isn't going to be easy,' and knowing we're going to get to that point, I think that's what he does best. He forces us to find a solution to our problems as a coach should, rather than just providing us with solutions on how to get there."

When asked what she was most grateful for, Misty said this: "Oh my gosh, that's really easy. I'm able to sit alongside a group of people that I trust and that I can be super proud of. We've all cheered each other on to these greater things, and are accomplishing them, even though they get clouded by all of the greater things still to be accomplished. When I think about who we were before the relocation, it blows my mind to think of where we are now as individuals and as a team. I can proudly say I work for Chick-fil-A on Archer Road.

"When people ask, 'What's the best part about your job?' I can easily say it's the people I get to work with. I'm also grateful that I am able to do my job, and mostly only my job, because now everybody else is doing their job. That was one of the first conversations I had with Gary, when he asked, 'Why are you doing that? That's not your job.' I replied, 'Well, somebody's gotta do it.' Now they understand what their jobs are from job descriptions, they own their jobs, and they want to do their best. Recently I was preparing for a three-week mission trip to Haiti with Triumph Community Ministries. I was stressing out about all that needed to be done before I left. Our team rallied behind me. Laura helped me get organized and Ryan covered for me while I was away. Being able to focus on my own job but knowing there are people that can allow me to leave for three weeks is reassuring." The reason the team can function at this level of leadership is because they have learned and applied the nine essentials of executive leadership: define reality, execute a vision, communicate more effectively, create an environment of anticipation, measure to track progress, train and support leadership, execute with excellence, celebrate victories, learn from mistakes.

As the team looks toward the future, they're using the lessons they've learned from our coaching sessions to move toward goals. They've learned the value of trust, accountability, faith, and clear communication, but they know their work isn't done. When it comes to self-discovery and our relationships with other people, the work is never done. I've seen real growth in them and positive outcomes in the business, and they are passing on all that they've learned to the people around them. What they've done is something that can be replicated by others with a passion to do better and be better. I hope that you've found outlined in these pages a strategy for yourself; with a willingness to work hard, push yourself beyond your comfort zone and ask the difficult questions, the possibilities are endless.

You will have some of the same sentiments as the Israelites did when they returned from exile:

"When the LORD brought back his exiles to Jerusalem,

it was like a dream!

We were filled with laughter,

and we sang for joy.

And the other nations said,

"What amazing things the LORD has done for them."

Yes, the LORD has done amazing things for us!
What joy!"

Psalms 126:1-3, NLT

Did you notice, "like a dream?" Did you notice, "filled with laughter", "sang with joy", "amazing things," "what joy!" This is what we experience when dreams come true.

★ ★ ★

"We each have an 'internal society.' If we know how to follow the path we can uncover the mysteries that lie in our mind and heart—and that of another person."

—*Gary L. Crawford*
In Celebration of Love, Marriage, and Sex

Questions for Personal and Professional Impact
- How does coaching provide a model for endless self-discovery?
- How does self-discovery enhance leadership?
- How might their coaching experience open doors of opportunity for the future?

"Every positive change in your life begins with a clear, unequivocal decision that you are going to either do something or stop doing something."

—*Anonymous*

Epilogue

"There are some people who live in a dream world, and there are some who face reality; and then there are those who turn one into the other."

— *Douglas H. Everett*

For CFA Gainesville-Archer Road, 2019 ended with a strong, focused team and financial goals that were exceeded by 140 percent, and according to the owner the organizational expectations were exceeded by 150 percent. In addition, Joe Wendling has been accepted into the corporate Leadership Development Plan, which will result in his becoming a future owner. Significant steps have been taken toward the second store.

Owner Ray Holloway and the team made a decision to move the coaching culture deeper into the organization by making two significant decisions: First, the Director Team will continue to focus on coaching principles as they lead into the future, as well as continuing to implement the policies, procedures, and strategies that have enabled such success thus far. Second, Ryan, as the executive director, will continue the coaching process. Ray and the team have selected five new additional directors as a "second team" to engage the coaching process. This second team consists of Selvin Rodriguez, Brad Dreffer, Hunter Good, and Tiesha Adams. Since these newly designated directors had effectively demonstrated the Seven Cs, it enabled them to be promoted to their new position.

The coaching relationship will allow them to fast track their own personal and professional growth and promote the coaching culture through the entire organization. At the time of this writing, the second-team coaching results over two short months have been stellar. They too, have clarified their purpose, are beginning to set SMART goals, develop a strategy, build trust, and lead others using the coach approach. It is expected that this team will not only strengthen the business and move them toward adding a second store, but will also produce future owner-operators as well.

Even though the same effective coaching principles will be used with the two distinct teams, each team has its own personality and group dynamics according to gifting and team chemistry. It's exciting to see how well the coaching process works every time and with everyone when you have a person or team genuinely ready to engage the process.

The power of coaching is reinforced by the fact that in 2018-2019 I used the same approach to lead a church revitalization. Among other extraordinary outcomes, this church experienced more numerical growth than the previous six years, placed eleven short-term mission teams on the field, provided the financial resources to pay their property mortgage and committed $1,000,000 to support a newly developed three-year growth plan.

In addition, Amazon Vision Ministries, a mission work that I co-founded with businessman Joe Fincher some twenty years ago, used the same approach to place ten teams in the west Amazon basin of Brazil. AVM continues to bring the Good News of the gospel, provide medical and dental care, conduct leadership training, and plant churches within the Ribeirinhos (river people) and indigenous people groups. One of many statements that Joe often references, and that I value, is, "Proper prior planning 💡 prevents poor performance, produces a pay-day, and promotes prosperity." I would add "and protects personal relationships."

Moreover, I used the same approach in creating a new missions entity Global Missions 365, now with twelve partnerships in seven countries. This work is led by my wife Ingrid as executive director and two gifted team members, Michael Justice and Melissa Allen.

As one person recently observed after reading the leadership missions year-end report. "You are to be affirmed for an amazing year! Reading through the highlights of your year was like watching a highlight reel of nothing but Super Bowl plays. You've done more in a year than I will do in a lifetime. Proud of you and celebrating the great good that was done in 2019!"

"Success is not about your resources. It's about how resourceful you are with what you have."

— *Tony Robbins*

I give credit first to Jesus Christ for His grace and wisdom and the One who asked more questions than He answered. According to Martin B. Copenhaver, "In the Gospels Jesus asks many more questions than He answers. To be precise, in the Bible, Jesus asks 307 questions. He is asked 183, of which he only answers 3."

Asking questions was central to Jesus's life and teachings. You might even say He used the coach approach in His teaching and leading personal and organizational transformation (Copenhaver 2014).

"Not to us, Lord, not to us
but to your name be the glory,
because of your love and faithfulness."

— *Psalm 115:1*

Second, to the powerful coach approach that helps us find our dreams and live them. Third, to a wonderful group of people to work with.

As I said in the preface of this book, "Dreams drive us. But dreams don't just happen. They are realized by knowing and having the will to implement the principles that are non-negotiable. The principles empower our dreams to come true." As Christopher Reeve stated, "So many dreams at first seem impossible. And then they seem improbable. And then when we summon the will, they soon become inevitable."

What is your dream? No matter where you are now, no matter what seems improbable or impossible, go within yourself, claim or reclaim that dream and pursue it. The most important thing is to find your God-given dream, identify His purpose for your life, realize your passion, and "live bravely and gallantly."

"The only thing that will stop you from fulfilling your dreams is you."
— *Tom Bradley*

Questions for Personal and Professional Impact
- How has coaching affected the "bottom line" and the quality of the work environment within the company?
- How is coaching applicable for other areas of life and business?
- What is your dream and what is the one most brave decision you can make now to see it come true?

As I have shared with you, Mrs. Woodley, my high-school science teacher, believed in me. With one hand on my shoulder, and one simple statement of confidence in me, she led me to the empowering decision, "I *can* do better." That redirected my life!

Let this story of dreams-come-true be the hand on your shoulder and the statement of confidence in your ability that will lead you to the one decision that will take you from "there to anywhere!"

One other thing. Decide now to passionately pursue your dream and don't look back. As you read earlier, there is a difference in being interested and being committed.

The Vikings were known for "burning their ships." If you have read much about this, you know it was basically for three reasons: one was to announce their presence, striking fear and panic in the enemy. Another was to clarify that the only way home was to win the battle. Finally, it was to make a clear statement that they were fully committed to seeing their dream come true.

Alexander the Great did the same when he led a fleet of Greek and Macedonian ships into Asia Minor.

U.S. President George Washington did a similar thing when he burned all the boats along the Delaware at a pivotal moment of battle.

The music group King and Country produced a song entitled, "Burn the Ship." The song stems from a battle that Luke Smallbone's wife, Courtney, faced with an addiction to prescribed medication. The lyrics read:

Burn the ships, cut the ties
Send a flare into the night
Say a prayer, turn the tide
Dry your tears and wave goodbye
Step into a new day
We can rise up from the dust and walk away
We can dance upon our heartache, yeah
So light a match, leave the past, burn the ships
And don't you look back.

A wall poster says, "In war, he who is ready to die wins."

The point is this. Pursuing your dreams is a battle. Business is a battle. Life is a battle—yet it is full of hopes and dreams. One thing I have learned and been reminded of many times, there is no forward movement without a decision and a commitment.

Decide now! Burn the ship! This is how dreams come true!

"What is not started today is never finished tomorrow."

— *Johann Wolfgang von Goethe*

Appendix I
Organizational Structure

Operator

|

Directors

(Talent/Marketing/Facilities/Drive-Through/Guest Experience/
Heart of House/Executive)

|

Supervisors

|

Leaders

|

Team Members

Vision:

To provide our guests and our team with a 5-star experience by excelling in every part of the business and strengthening the Chick-fil-A brand everywhere to the point that our guests, Chick-fil-A corporate, and other Chick-fil-A stores want to visit and see what we are doing.

Mission:

A culture of unity, collaborating together with the same end in mind, excelling at the highest level in:

- "Remark"able Service
- "Crave"able Food
- Blazing Speed
- Bulls-eye Accuracy
- Hospital Cleanliness
- Increasing Sales
- Growing Profits
- Consistent Development of People

Values:
- Character
- Chemistry
- Integrity
- Servant Spirit
- Reliability
- Genuine
- Urgency
- Learner

Appendix II
Leadership Training Track for
Chick-fil-A Archer Road

We're not just in the chicken **business**, we're in the **people business**. I live in a do-it-yourself world. If you wish to enrich days, plant flowers; If you wish to enrich years, plant trees; If you wish to enrich Eternity, plant ideals in the lives of others. – Truett Cathy

Foundations of Flagship – Session Topics

Session 1: **Foundations**

- Who is Chick-fil-A as a company?

Session 2: **The Flagship**

- Who is Chick-fil-A Archer Road?

Session 3: **Exploration**

- Who am I?

Session 4: **Discovery**

- What do I believe?

Session 5: **Make the Call**

- Judgement Calls & Guest and Team Recovery

Session 6: **Where's the map?**

- Scheduling & SMART Goals

Session 7: **Building Leaders**

- Coaching Culture

Session 8: **Grab the Wheel**

- Ownership & Conviction

Session 9: **Engine Room**

- Self-assurance & confidence using the tools

Session 10: **Where to next?**

- Celebration & Reflection

"You want to be great? *SERVE.*

You want to be first? *GO LAST.*

You want to be promoted? *HUMBLE YOURSELF.*"

– Pastor Joey Martin

Appendix III
Leadership Development Guide

Leadership Development Guide

We are answering the QUESTIONS

Where are we now?
Where do we want to go?
What do we do to get there?

The FACTORS of increasing performance

Performance Management Plan
Trust and accountability for authority and empowerment
Increase leadership capacity at all levels
Increase communication and collaboration
Enhance training and development

The AREAS of the plan

Strategy - common purpose and direction
Structure - align with strategy
Process - collaboration
Rewards - capture energy and motivation

A LEADER is one who has

- ✓ A clarified vision
- ✓ A high relationship quotient
- ✓ A personal growth plan
- ✓ An understanding of business finance
- ✓ The ability to execute with excellence
- ✓ Reproduces other leaders

Core VALUES

- _____
- _____
- _____

GaryCrawfordLeadership.com

Appendix IV
B.R.I.D.G.E.

A team of servant leaders who are in clear alignment with the values of Chick-fil-A Archer Road and are constantly focused on the care of our Guests, Team and Brand Recognition/Solidification/Growth in our community. This is a team of individuals that consistently exemplifies high character and strive to create a flagship experience through outreach and service by engaging the heart.

- **B- Build** strong and open lines of communication among all team members and throughout all levels of leadership. You will be a voice of positive and comprehensive communication.

- **R- Represent** Chick-fil-A Archer Road by being committed to participating in community events and Chick-fil-A sponsored events & staff meetings.

- **I- Inspire** positivity and good will as you ALWAYS lead by example inside and outside of the store. The community will recognize you as members of the Chick-fil-A brand and a valuable member of our community. Our goal is to serve other individuals, organizations and businesses in a way that creates a chain reaction of kindness.

- **D- Discern** personal and professional needs and wishes of those around you. Constantly communicating ways that we may best support our team and guests in every area of life.

- **G- Grow** continually, personally and professionally. Be dedicated to reading, asking questions, establishing a Coaching Culture as well as be willing to take part in the necessary training to effectively perform marketing and brand growth events.

- **E- Engage** and empower our entire team, cultivating a sense of community and family. This team will plan and execute team outings, contests and appreciation initiatives.

Appendix V
A Personal Growth Plan

REACH YOUR POTENTIAL
"IMAGINE, EVALUATE, ACT"

"Unless commitment is made, there are only promises and hopes,
but no plan." – Peter Drucker

Influence Others

| PURPOSE | VISION | MISSION | VALUES |

FOUNDATION

"I find it fascinating that most people plan their vacations with more care than they plan their lives. Perhaps that is because it is easier to escape than to change." – Jim Rohn

Appendix VI
Developing a Coaching Culture

Developing a Coaching Culture

> Coaching is an approach to dialogue – it's a role, mindset, or skillset for positive outcomes.

A coaching culture *provides*
- ✓ openness
- ✓ curiosity
- ✓ trust
- ✓ inspiration
- ✓ innovation
- ✓ growth

> Coaching requires *strong relationships* an *powerful conversations*.

Coaching culture benefits include
- ❖ increased honesty and trust
- ❖ leadership development
- ❖ motivation
- ❖ change management
- ❖ retention
- ❖ stronger vendor and customer relationships
- ❖ personal and team growth

> Developing a coaching culture requires a clear vision, a strategy, strong senior leadership, team commitment, communication and behavior changes.

Strategy
- ➢ Understanding and commitment from senior leadership
- ➢ Casting Vision and consistantly restating the vision
- ➢ Communicate the strategy
- ➢ Garner collaboration and engagement
- ➢ Teach coaching skills
- ➢ Long-term commitment to coaching routines
- ➢ Develop an assessment
- ➢ Evaluate the program
- ➢ Engage a coach to train the team in coaching practices

Appendix VII
Leadership Evaluation Rubric

Values Evaluation Rubric

Leadership in large measure is a collection of judgement calls. This Rubric is meant to help guide our team through these calls in the restaurant with a specific focus on leadership development and alignment with our store's core values. In each decision, we are shooting to satisfy the guest, honor the business, empower the team and share/recreate the decision.

Candidate Name: _____

Position candidate is applying/eligible for: _____

The candidate will be evaluated on the following scale:

Character
1   2   3   4   5

Example: _____
Growth Opportunity: _____

Servant Spirit
1   2   3   4   5

Example: _____
Growth Opportunity: _____

Urgency
1   2   3   4   5

Example: _____
Growth Opportunity: _____

Learner
1   2   3   4   5

Example: _____
Growth Opportunity: _____

Honesty
1   2   3   4   5

Integrity
1   2   3   4   5

Example: _____
Growth Opportunity: _____

Ownership
1   2   3   4   5

Example: _____
Growth Opportunity: _____

Accountability
1   2   3   4   5

Example: _____
Growth Opportunity: _____

Reliable
1   2   3   4   5

Example: _____
Growth Opportunity: _____

Genuine
1   2   3   4   5

Works Cited

Cathy, S. Truett. *Eat More Chikin: Inspire More People.* Looking Glass Books, 2002.
https://www.chick-fil-a.com/about/history

Copenhaver, Martin. *Jesus Is the Question: The 307 Questions Jesus Asked and the 3 He Answered.* Abingdon Press, 2014.

Greiner, Nadine. "Making the Business Case for Executing Coaching." Association for Talent development. August 29, 2018. https://www.td.org/insights/making-the-business-case-for-executive-coaching

Haverluck, Michael F. "Chick-fil-A Now #3 Restaurant Chain in U.S." June 21, 2019. https://onenewsnow.com/business/2019/06/21/chick-fil-a-now-3-restaurant-chain-in-us

Levin, Marissa. "8 Ways to Build a Culture of Trust Based on Harvard's Neuroscience." Inc.com. October 5, 2017.
https://www.inc.com/marissa-levin/harvard-neuroscience-research-reveals-8-ways-to-build-a-culture-of-trust.html.

Lewis, C.S. *The Reading Life: The Joy of Seeing New Worlds Through Others' Eyes.* HarperOne, 2019.

Miner, Karen. "The Real Reason Chick-fil-A is Closed on Sunday." September 27, 2016. https://www.mashed.com/25923/real-reason-chick-fil-closed-sundays/?utm_campaign=clip.

Oches, Sam. "The Truth about Chick-fil-A's Drive-Thru." *QSR Magazine*, October 16, 2019.

Taylor, Kate. "Chick-fil-A likely Loses Out on More Than $1 Billion in Sales Every Year by Closing on Sundays." *Business Insider,* July 29, 2019.

Trombetta, Sadie. "What Does Reading Do to Your Brain? These Five Effects Are Pretty Astounding." August 11, 2017. https://www.bustle.com/profile/sadie-trombetta-1909289.

Vigliotti, Jake. "The Untold Truth of Chick-fil-A." November 30, 2016 (updated May 15, 2019). https://www.mashed.com/32659/10-things-didnt-know-chik-fil/.

Reading Recommendations

HalfTime
By Bob Buford
This is the book that originally inspired me to explore how coaching could enrich my life, and how I could invest in others using the coach approach.

The Servant: A Simple Story About the True Essence of Leadership
By James C. Hunter
Several of the directors reference the epiphany they had when they learned the difference between leading with power and leading with authority. This book is the source of that wisdom, and I share it with all my coachees.

Strengthsfinder 2.0
By Tom Rath
This book encourages readers to diagnose their strengths and work from there, embracing their natural talents rather than struggling to overcome their deficits.

The Speed of Trust

By Stephen M.R. Covey

Covey makes the case that trust is "the one thing that changes everything." He also states that the higher the trust, the greater the speed of progress. You can't have success without trust.

Caring Enough to Confront: How to Understand and Express Your Deepest Feelings Toward Others

By David Augsburger

Augsburger teaches the reader how to build trust, cope with blame and prejudice, and be honest about anger and frustration.

The Oz Principle

By Roger Commons, Tom Smith, and Craig Hickman

The authors state that personal, professional, and organizational results improve drastically when people recognize and avoid the traps of the victim mentality and establish accountability.

The One Thing

By Gary Keller

The author raise the question, "What's the one thing you can do that day?" Doing everything else would be easier and unnecessary—the one thing that will move forward everything of importance. A powerful concept to apply in order to help you focus on what matters the most. The "one thing" will move forwad everything of importance.

Awesomely Simple

By John Spence

John Spence says business success is simple but not easy. He provides strategy and tools for "turning ideas into action."

The Seven Habits of Highly Effective People

By Stephen R. Covey

This book is a one-of-a-kind guide to personal and professional change and success. The principles are eternal.

Wellbeing

By Tom Rath and Jim Harter

Providing insight into how you can "enjoy each day and get more out of your life," the authors lay out the five essential elements of wellbeing: career, social, financial, physical, and community.

Boundaries

By Dr. Henry McCloud and Dr. John Townsend

Simply put, this book teaches us when to say yes and how to say no in both our personal and professional lives.

About the Author

D r. Gary Crawford is a visionary leader. Originally trained in science as a biologist, in pursuit of his ministry calling he graduated from Southwestern Seminary with his M. Div. and D.Min. Having served at Westside Baptist Church in Gainesville, Florida, he now holds emeritus status. Dr. Crawford has served on the following boards: International Mission Board of the Southern Baptist Convention, Baptist College of Florida, and State Board of Missions of the Florida Baptist Convention. He is the founder of Gary Crawford Leadership, through which he engages in leadership coaching that empowers transformational personal and professional growth.

Dr. Gary Crawford is the visionary and co-founder of Amazon Vision Ministries, which works in the west Amazon basin of Brazil. He is also the founder of Global Missions 365. He and his wife,

Ingrid, who serves as Executive Director, are in various levels of partnership with twelve ministries in seven countries.

Gary Crawford is a proven leader who has led organizations nationally and internationally, from 100 to 4,000 people, in areas of personal and organizational growth.

❖ **Staying Power**: A leader with staying power—exceeding the national average tenure of a senior pastor by a factor of 10.

❖ **Inspires**: A leader who has inspired more than 150 people to full-time missionary/pastoral positions across the nation and around the world.

❖ **Delegator**: A skilled delegator who consistently developed staff.

❖ **Strategist**: A strategist who understood the need to anticipate the future, plan for the future, and staff for the future.

❖ **Teacher**: A dedicated teacher who knows ultimately the leader is the lesson.

❖ **Mediator**: A practiced mediator in conflict resolution.

❖ **Servant**: A leader who loves those he serves and leads.

❖ **Communicator**: An experienced communicator who seeks to understand first, then to be understood.

Gary Crawford continues to provide expertise in:

❖ Long-range strategic planning

- ❖ Mentoring and relationship-building
- ❖ Consensus-building to develop momentum
- ❖ Deploying existing staff to handle new challenges
- ❖ Identifying and addressing areas of weakness
- ❖ Organizational transitions
- ❖ Fundraising—13 initiatives, raising more than $27 million
- ❖ Clarifying and managing expectations
- ❖ Raising new leaders from the existing organization
- ❖ Problem solving, small to large issues and opportunities
- ❖ Understanding proper organizational design
- ❖ Recognizing when/where new leaders are needed
- ❖ Discernment of "timing" for personal and organizational decisions

Gary Crawford
WEBSITE: garycrawfordleadership.com
Twitter: @garycrawford
Facebook: @garycrawfordleadership
LinkedIn: Linkedin.com/in/Dr-Gary-Crawford

MISSIONS ORGANIZATIONS
Global Missions 365
GlobalMissions365.org
Facebook: @GlobalMissions365

Amazon Vision Ministries

www.amazonvisionministries.com

Facebook: @AmazonVisionMinistries

Thoughts About the Coach

Gary Crawford is a man of high integrity. Does that sum it up? He does what he says, when he says, how he says. He cares, and you can tell how much he cares for others. I think what he does best is—he's very relational, so he can make you feel at ease. You feel comfortable confiding in him. He asks a lot of good questions, really thought-provoking questions. He leads us well through questions.

— Ray Holloway

One of the things that he does best is asking the tough questions. He asks them relentlessly until he gets an answer. Even if they are the tough questions and even if you're having a tough time getting the answer, you won't stop the conversation until the answer is found, somehow, some way. That's something that I didn't expect going in. He's just relentless.

—Joe Wendling

Who is Gary Crawford? He is a genuine person who cares about people's outcomes and what he can do to help them. He asks really good questions...he'll follow up with another question to help us figure out the answer. He did such a good job. He was so interested in us and involved in us.

— TJ Graham

He has been by far the most trustworthy influence on the growth of our team; he is the voice that everyone trusted even though we didn't know him. He brought the proof to the table in speaking with love and grace and gentleness.

— Misty Emerson

He frames our lives in a way that's different, in a way that pushes us to be better. That is who Gary is. Someone who's invested in not only his own life and journey, but others' lives and journeys. At the beginning he said, this is not going to be easy. I think it's what he does best, forces us to find a solution to our problems as a coach should, rather than providing us with just solutions on how to get there.

— Ryan Summers

He's inspirational. He's got a mindset that thinks outside the box. He doesn't let you off the hook.

— Laura Wisener

Other Books by Gary L. Crawford

In Celebration of *Love, Marriage, and Sex*

L ove backs us into a corner. It asks for everything we have. And nowhere does love work more deeply than in marriage. Marriage is about exposure. It is truth between two people, and it is about the opportunity to know and to be known. Sex is the handiwork of love and the tool of marriage. It is sacred ground, a gift filled with beauty, grace, and power. Song of Solomon demonstrates with beauty, reverence, and clarity the celebration of love, marriage, and sex. It offers practical and reliable guidelines for these essentials and more:

- Decisions about dating
- Choosing a spouse
- Keeping romance in marriage
- Making and celebrating memories
- Leaving a legacy for family

Nowhere do we find a more relevant word about these important matters, nor a more beautiful portrait of celebration, than in this poetic expression of God's gift in the Song of Solomon.

Endorsement

"Dr. Gary Crawford knows that in the face of threats and challenges to the marriage and family structure of society, there is a clear and present need to know principles of strong, loving, and meaningful marriage and to provide guidance in putting them into practice. His thoughts flow carefully, joyfully, and powerfully from his reading of the Song of Solomon and his personal experience in marriage to his own true love. As a sociologist and Christian, I heartily recommend this book to all of those who are dating, who are contemplating marriage, who want to sustain romance and commitment in a marriage, and who seek to build a family legacy for the succeeding generations."

— Ronald L. Akers, Ph.D.
Professor of Sociology and Criminology
University of Florida

Grieving: My Pilgrimage of Love: Engaging Grief for Healing and Hope

"This book encourages because the end result is that there is meaning to life—all of it."

— Governor Mike Huckabee

Endorsement

"*Grieving: My Pilgrimage of Love*, the latest book from the fertile mind of Pastor Gary Crawford, is a story that brings the tributaries of life to flow as one river. That river is love. When that love is gone from our presence, the river still flows but often cuts a new course. The new course must include healing and hope, or the purpose for the river is lost. This is a fascinating read; Pastor Gary feels and writes with the same ink."

— Dr. John Sullivan
Executive Director—Treasurer Emeritus
Florida Baptist Convention

Story Terrace